A GUIDE TO SUPERVISING NON-NATIVE ENGLISH WRITERS OF THESES AND DISSERTATIONS

Focused on the writing process, *A Guide to Supervising Non-native English Writers of Theses and Dissertations* presents approaches that can be employed by supervisors to help address the writing issues or difficulties that may emerge during the provisional and confirmation phases of the thesis/dissertation journey. Pre-writing advice and post-writing feedback that can be given to students are explained and illustrated.

A growing number of students who are non-native speakers of English are enrolled in Masters and PhD programmes at universities across the world where English is the language of communication. These students often encounter difficulties when writing a thesis or dissertation in English – primarily, understanding the requirements and expectations of the new academic context and the conventions of academic writing.

Designed for easy use by supervisors, this concise guide focuses specifically on the relationship between reading for and preparing to write the various parts or chapters; the creation of argument; making and evaluating claims, judgements and conclusions; writing coherent and cohesive text; meeting the generic and discipline-specific writing conventions; designing conference abstracts and PowerPoint presentations; and writing journal articles.

John Bitchener is Professor of Applied Linguistics, Auckland University of Technology, New Zealand.

A GUIDE TO SUPERVISING NON-NATIVE ENGLISH WRITERS OF THESES AND DISSERTATIONS

Focusing on the Writing Process

John Bitchener

NEW YORK AND LONDON

First published 2018
by Routledge
711 Third Avenue, New York, NY 10017

and by Routledge
2 Park Square, Milton Park, Abingdon, Oxon, OX14 4RN

Routledge is an imprint of the Taylor & Francis Group, an informa business

© 2018 Taylor & Francis

The right of John Bitchener to be identified as author of this work
has been asserted by him in accordance with sections 77 and 78 of
the Copyright, Designs and Patents Act 1988.

All rights reserved. No part of this book may be reprinted or
reproduced or utilised in any form or by any electronic, mechanical,
or other means, now known or hereafter invented, including
photocopying and recording, or in any information storage or
retrieval system, without permission in writing from the publishers.

Trademark notice: Product or corporate names may be trademarks
or registered trademarks, and are used only for identification and
explanation without intent to infringe.

Library of Congress Cataloging in Publication Data
A catalog record for this book has been requested

ISBN: 978-0-415-63180-8 (hbk)
ISBN: 978-0-415-63181-5 (pbk)
ISBN: 978-0-203-09648-2 (ebk)

Typeset in Bembo
by Book Now Ltd, London

Printed and bound by CPI Group (UK) Ltd, Croydon, CR0 4YY

CONTENTS

Preface	*vii*
Acknowledgements	*ix*

1	Introduction	1
2	Advice and Feedback in the Provisional Enrolment Period	8
3	Advice on the Selection of Content for Dissertation Chapters	37
4	Feedback on the Selection of Content for Dissertation Chapters	54
5	Advice and Feedback on the Creation of Argument in Dissertation Chapters	74
6	Advice or Feedback on the Coherence of Dissertation Arguments	89
7	Advice and Feedback on the Writing of Other Texts during the Dissertation Journey	101

vi Contents

Appendices

Appendix A	*Some Key Aspects of the Published Research Informing the Focus of this Book*	*119*
Appendix B	*Code of Practice for Supervisors and Student Responsibilities*	*130*
Appendix C	*Sample 20-Minute PowerPoint Slide Presentation*	*134*
Appendix D	*Typical Guidelines for the Submission of Manuscripts to Journals for Publication*	*154*
Appendix E	*Some of the Typical Reasons Journal Editors Reject Manuscripts before Seeking Reviews*	*156*
References		*158*
Index		*161*

PREFACE

The Aim and Overall Structure of the Book

The primary aim of this book is to suggest approaches (pre-writing advice and post-writing feedback) that supervisors can consider adopting to help their non-native students overcome some of the more recurrent writing challenges they may encounter when writing a thesis or dissertation in English. (Hereafter, the word 'dissertation' will be used rather than 'thesis' even though the book is as relevant to writers of theses as it is to those writing dissertations.) The *pre-writing advice* that supervisors can give their students before they start writing will help minimise the writing issues or difficulties they may experience as much as it may reduce the amount of *post-writing feedback* they need to give. Writing challenges may be particular to the writing of different parts of a dissertation as well as generic and recurrent across different parts (sections or chapters) of a dissertation.

Following the introductory chapter, Chapter 2 considers some of the challenges that may occur during the provisional period of enrolment before confirmation of candidature. Chapters 3–6 focus on those that students may encounter when writing the various chapters of their dissertation. In particular, Chapter 3 provides advice on the selection of content for each of the dissertation chapters and Chapter 4 suggests areas of feedback that may need to be provided by supervisors on the content that students have included in their texts. Chapter 5 considers both the advice and feedback that supervisors may wish to consider with regard to the creation of argument. This is followed in Chapter 6 with advice and feedback on how to ensure that the arguments throughout the dissertation are coherent. While being related to the writing of a dissertation, Chapter 7 provides guidance for overcoming some of the challenges that students can encounter when preparing written texts for conferences (e.g. abstracts, PowerPoint slides for presentation) and publications (e.g. journal articles).

viii Preface

Reasons for the Book and Its Intended Audience

Several reasons informed the writing of this book. First, the growing number of migrant and international student enrolments in dissertation writing programmes in English-medium universities across the globe has meant that non-native writers of English may encounter a range of challenges as they seek to understand a new learning context (often with different epistemological roots and approaches to gaining and disseminating knowledge), and a new writing genre (the research-informed dissertation) with characteristics that may be different to those they are familiar with. Second, some non-native student writers may believe that they have an understanding of the requirements and expectations of the new discourse community but discover in their early weeks of enrolment that their assumptions and expectations do not always align with those of the academic community they have entered. Third, the challenges that are identified and addressed in this book are not necessarily those that only non-native student writers may encounter: native student writers may have a greater knowledge of what is expected (given that they have already studied in an English-medium university) but this does not mean that they have the skill to apply their head knowledge. It is not an uncommon lament by supervisors that their native writers of English don't know how to write accurately and coherently.

With an increasing multilingual population of graduate students seeking qualifications that require the completion of a dissertation, the demand for an increasing number of supervisors, who are able to supervise students from a non-native English background, is reaching a critical point in many universities around the world. This raises the question about how well equipped the supervisors are to meet this need. Universities typically provide some form of training for their new supervisors but so often this focuses more on university processes and procedures than on the knowledge and skills that supervisors need if they are to meet the diverse challenges that their non-native students may encounter. Some institutions offer seminars and workshops for supervisors but often these are attended by only a small proportion of supervisors because they are optional rather than mandatory. Thus, this book seeks to provide some guidance for supervisors working with non-native students writing a dissertation. Supervisors may be overseeing a range of dissertation types nowadays so it is not possible, within the confines of a book such as this, to offer advice on all types or formats. Given that the preponderance of dissertations tend to be of the traditional format with an introduction, a literature review, a methodology chapter, a presentation of results chapter, a discussion of results chapter and a conclusion, the book has been designed to focus on this pattern of organisation. However, the material presented in Chapters 2–6 can easily be modified and adapted for formats that may be a little different (e.g. those that combine results and discussion, those that combine discussion and conclusion or those that have more than one literature review chapter).

ACKNOWLEDGEMENTS

I am indebted to a number of people who have played a role in my thinking, research and writing on the supervision of both native and non-native writers of theses and dissertations written in English. Without the highs and lows of supervision, I would not have been able to write a book such as this, so I am indeed grateful to all the doctoral and Masters students who have forced me to reflect on better ways to help them understand and apply what the academic community of scholars, researchers, examiners and editors expect of research and reporting at the graduate and postgraduate levels. Without the feedback from co-researchers, journal and book editors and reviewers, conference delegates and university colleagues, the pre-writing advice and post-writing feedback discussed in this book would not have been as extensive and as practically oriented as it is. As always, I am extremely grateful for the wonderful support, guidance and patience of my editor at Routledge, Naomi Silverman, and the whole editorial and production team. Last, but not least, I wish to thank my partner, Edwin Cheong, and our friends for their on-going interest in the development of the book.

1

INTRODUCTION

In the Preface of this book, the aims and overall structure of the book were discussed, together with an explanation of why the book was considered necessary and who the intended reader was expected to be. Against this background, Chapter 1 begins with a consideration of the writing challenges that non-native dissertation students can encounter and why this may be the case. The chapter then proceeds to outline the approach that is taken in this book to help supervisors address the writing challenges of their non-native students. It explains that the provision of pre-writing advice and post-writing feedback are the two key ways in which supervisors typically instruct students about what is expected of them in the writing of their dissertation. Advice and feedback are discussed in terms of (1) what is meant by each of these approaches, (2) who gives the advice and feedback, (3) when the advice and feedback are given and (4) the content of the advice and feedback that is typically given. Thus the aim of this introductory chapter is to establish the type of content that the following chapters will provide.

The Writing Challenges that Non-native Dissertation Students Can Encounter

Over the past 15–20 years, a body of literature (see Appendix A for a summary of some of the key empirical research) has reported on the writing issues that supervisors have identified as problematic for both native and non-native writers of dissertations in English (e.g. Basturkmen, East & Bitchener, 2014; Bitchener, 2016; Bitchener & Basturkmen, 2006; Bitchener, Basturkmen & East, 2010; Cadman, 1997; Casanave & Hubbard, 1992; Cooley & Lewkowicz, 1995, 1997; Dong, 1998; Hyland, 2007). Specifically, the research has commented on

2 Introduction

writing difficulties (a) at the sentence level (e.g. grammatical and lexical errors), (b) at the paragraph and wider discourse level (e.g. coherence, cohesion, creation of argument), (c) in observing genre characteristics (e.g. achieving discourse move expectations, effective organisation and rhetorical structuring of academic argument), (d) in offering a level of criticality, (e) in justifying an individual stance or position and (f) in presenting theoretical and empirical justifications for claims and conclusions). In a recent publication, Bitchener (2016) refers to several additional challenges that supervisors in New Zealand and Australian universities say they need to respond to in their students' dissertation writing: (a) discussing the results of their research in light of the big picture established in the literature review chapter(s); (b) drawing upon the methodology of other studies to explain divergent findings and on their own methodology to explain their findings; (c) referring to theoretical perspectives to explain their research findings; (d) writing coherent arguments/justifications; and (e) using source material appropriately and effectively. On the other hand, student accounts of difficulty (East, Bitchener & Basturkmen, 2012) report that these are oriented more towards difficulties and uncertainty in their use of academic and general English and in their ability to use the literature for its various purposes in different parts of the dissertation (e.g. to introduce the research, to justify the problem focus, to explain their findings and to justify their claims and conclusions). That non-native students encounter difficulties or challenges in these areas of their dissertation writing begs the question about why this is the case.

Why Do Some Non-native Writers Encounter Dissertation-Writing Challenges?

Recent migrants and international students who have not previously studied in an English-medium context may have had prior learning and teaching experiences that are different to those that native-writing students have had. Thus, the knowledge they have gained in former educational contexts may be different to that taught in English-medium contexts. Sometimes this is a result of different epistemological understandings of what constitutes appropriate knowledge and practice. On the other hand, they may not have had much experience in applying the knowledge they have been taught before enrolling in an English-medium university. They may enter the dissertation programme with assumptions about what is expected and, upon realising that some of them are not observed in the new learning context, become anxious and struggle to re-learn what is required and expected by the new academic community. Students in this situation are often more dependent upon their supervisors for explicit knowledge and guidance. This is something that, at doctoral level in particular, is not expected by some supervisors. However, the reality is that gaps in knowledge and experience need to be filled one way or another. The burden is typically placed on the primary supervisor who may have a tacit knowledge

Introduction **3**

of what is expected but not an explicit knowledge that they can communicate to their students. This raises the question, then, about the extent to which the needs of supervisors are met by their institutions.

Approaches to Overcoming the Writing Challenges of Non-native Dissertation Students

At the institutional level, a range of learning support services are typically available for students (e.g. one-to-one and small group sessions) as well as seminars and/or workshops on various aspects of designing and carrying out research and on writing it up as a dissertation, but support services for supervisors tend to be more limited in terms of both availability and level of training that explains explicitly what is expected and how the expectations can be met. The aim of this book, then, is to suggest approaches that may help meet this need. The pre-writing advice and the post-writing feedback that are given in the following chapters is intended to provide supervisors with hands-on approaches they can adopt when giving advice and feedback on each of the dissertation chapters.

Pre-writing Advice and Post-writing Feedback to Address the Writing Challenges of Non-native Dissertation Students

In undergraduate and graduate study, students typically receive explicit instruction in timetabled classes but when undertaking research for a dissertation, the primary form of instruction for most students is advice and feedback from supervisors. Some doctoral programmes require their students to take course-work classes for one or two years before starting a dissertation so, for these students, instruction may be given on what is expected and/or required when designing, conducting and writing up dissertation research. Students in other contexts may have received some form of instruction about expectations and/or requirements when writing a Masters level thesis. Because the nature of such instruction can vary from context to context, it is best not to assume anything and find out in early meetings with each student what they know and what experiences they have already had. In my own context, during the early discussions with a new doctoral student, pre-writing advice is typically given about a wide range of topics and this continues throughout the supervisory process, especially before students start a new aspect of their work (i.e. in both their research and in their writing up of the research). Post-writing feedback, on the other hand, is reactive. It comments on the strengths and weaknesses of what the student has written and typically leads to further advice about what should be focused on next. The following sub-sections of this chapter explain in more detail what is meant by pre-writing advice and post-writing feedback.

4 Introduction

Pre-writing Advice

What is Pre-writing Advice?

The term *pre-writing advice* can be used to refer to directives about what must be done, recommendations about what should be done or suggestions about options that students might do well to consider and act upon. Therefore, given the difference between mandatory and optional advice, advisors need, first of all, to be clear in their own mind about the extent to which they consider their advice to be mandatory or optional and then make sure that their students understand the difference and know what is expected and/or required with each piece of advice that is given. To some extent, the level of advice that is given will depend on factors such as who is giving it, when it is given, and what the advice is about.

Who Gives the Advice?

Advice may be given by anyone but, most frequently, it is given by the primary supervisor, other supervisors or advisors in the supervisory team, and, to a lesser extent, by learning support advisors/instructors, conference attendees, journal reviewers and doctoral peers. Most often, this advice is given in one-on-one meetings and exchanges but sometimes several members of the supervisory team will provide advice. University schools and departments sometimes have other meetings or events at which students are given advice. For example, at my university, students receive (a) formal advice from members of the faculty's doctoral board when it considers the readiness of a student to be confirmed as a doctoral candidate or (b) more informal advice from delegates when presenting aspects of their work at internal conferences or research days.

In my own case, because I am supervising a large number of doctoral students and many of them are researching in similar areas to one another, I hold monthly cohort and pot luck meetings. The cohort meetings enable me to give advice to the cohort of students about matters of common interest. Frequently, the focus of these meetings will be advice on (a) writing up different parts of the dissertation, (b) oral presentations of sections of their work, especially before presenting at conferences, (c) meeting faculty and/or university requirements and (d) the topics/issues that they are investigating. At these meetings, there is also an opportunity for members of the cohort to provide advice on the topics being discussed. The pot luck component of the meeting is a shared meal. Each student brings a plate of food or a dish to share. Very often the contributions are from their own ethnic background. This informal time together facilitates the exchange of on-going advice from both the supervisor and the students on a wide range of topics or issues. Thus, there can be many providers of advice.

When Is the Advice Given?

The short answer to this question is throughout the enrolment period. As primary supervisor, I believe it is important to give pre-writing advice to my students before they start any new written task. Failure to give carefully considered pre-writing advice before students embark on a new aspect of their work can mean that more time ends up being spent on post-writing feedback. This initial advice includes a discussion of what students know and what experiences they have had in relation to the task ahead. Generally speaking, I find that they need more advice at the early stages of their enrolment even though they often think that they know what is required. Later in this chapter, I outline some of the key areas I discuss with students in the early weeks and months as well as the types of advice that are typically provided.

What Advice Is Typically Given to Dissertation Students?

The type of advice that is given to students tends to depend on the stage of the journey they are at and the supervisor's understanding of what the student already knows and does not know. For example, it is most often the case that more advice, in the early stages, will be given on university and discipline expectations and requirements whereas advice that is given as students prepare to write a section or chapter of their dissertation will focus more on specific matters related to the part-genre or chapter they are preparing. For example, this advice will typically focus on clarifying the purpose of a chapter, the direction of the argument to be presented, the selection of content relevant to the chapter, and how the chapter can most effectively be organised to gain maximum rhetorical effect. Before the second and third iterations of a chapter are written, advice is often provided on more micro matters concerning the conventions expected by the discipline. In Chapter 3 of this book, I consider the pre-writing advice that is typically given on each of the key chapters of a dissertation and, in Chapter 4, I focus on the post-writing feedback that often needs to be provided on each of these chapters.

Post-writing Feedback

What Is Post-writing Feedback?

Feedback has been defined in a variety of ways over the years because its role and central activities can vary from context to context. At dissertation level, it can refer to written and oral comment on what students have done or written well and to what they might need to consider doing or writing next. The latter, in terms of writing, may involve adding to, deleting, modifying or amending what has been written so that the text more closely approximates the norms, values, expectations and requirements of the discipline in which

6 Introduction

the research is situated. The feedback may introduce new suggestions or ideas for the student to consider or it may refer to guidance and advice given earlier in pre-writing advice meetings and discussions with supervisors/advisors but which needs to be further attended to.

Who Gives the Feedback?

Written feedback can be a time-consuming activity so it is more often than not provided by those who have the primary responsibility for a student's progress, that is, the primary supervisor and members of the supervisory team. In my own context, I tend to provide the feedback first and then invite others in this team to add to what has been provided. Because other members of the supervisory team offer a special area of knowledge or expertise, they are more likely to provide written feedback on certain pieces of written text rather than on all pieces of a text in the early drafting stages. For example, statistical experts will provide feedback on relevant sections of the methodology and results chapters but not on the literature review chapters until the first full draft of the dissertation has been assembled. Those who have provided written feedback are always invited to a meeting with the student so that they can (a) check that the student has understood the feedback and (b) provide further explanation or clarification if necessary. It is sometimes the case that a feedback issue is difficult to explain in a manageable way on a student's text and that a detailed discussion is a more appropriate way to respond. While the supervisory team is more likely to provide feedback on the content of the student's text and on the way in which the content has been organised to create an argument, learning support centres are more likely to provide written feedback on academic writing and linguistic accuracy/appropriateness issues.

When Is the Feedback Given and What Is Its Focus?

Written feedback is provided as a response to a piece of text that a student has submitted. The text may be at different stages of development. First, students may submit notes in different forms to see what the supervisor thinks of their ideas before they convert this material into text. As I explain in the following chapters, my students are asked to submit, first, a detailed table of contents of what they intend to include in various sections of a chapter. Then I ask them to explain this outline to me so that they and I can see if they need to add or delete anything before proceeding further. More will be said about this in the following chapters.

Once students have completed the first full iteration of a major section (or sometimes, if the student is particularly able, this may be when a whole chapter has been completed), they are given feedback on macro areas such as the selection of content, the coherence of the argument and the appropriateness of supporting arguments, evidence and examples. A feedback meeting is then scheduled for the purpose of discussing further the issues that have been raised in the written feedback.

The second iteration is usually submitted at a later stage in the journey. For example, if the first iteration was a student's literature review, it would have been completed in the first year of enrolment and before the student's confirmation in the programme. This iteration, including a revision of the first iteration, is not submitted until the student has completed as comprehensive a reading programme as possible. This second iteration would then include the additional literature that the student had read since submitting the first iteration. I require that my students submit this second iteration before they start data collection so that they don't discover as they read further during or after the data collection process that they should have included another element in the study for which additional data would then be required.

The third iteration of the literature review chapter is not submitted until the student has analysed the data and written up the findings or results chapter. Once the findings have been determined, additional literature, relating to one or more findings, may need to be added to the literature review so that the finding(s) can be discussed in the discussion of results chapter. It is sometimes the case that parts of the literature review may need to be deleted or modified in some way as a result of the finding(s) that emerged from the analysis. Thus, the third iteration of the chapter is best completed after the findings have been described and before they are discussed.

Three iterations of the other chapters of a dissertation are also required. The timing and reasoning for this is discussed further in the following chapters. It should also be noted that between these iterations, some students may need to do more iterations of sections of a chapter before the three main iterations of the chapter are commented upon. For example, some students experience more difficulty with the creation of argument than others. If this is the case, I may provide additional feedback, both written and oral. In addition to the formal feedback on chapter sections and on full chapters, students will often receive feedback on short email or text questions that they have sent.

Thus, it can be seen that post-writing feedback is provided at different stages of the dissertation journey and that this depends on the chapter or part-genre of the dissertation being responded to. The advice and feedback approaches introduced in this chapter and described in detail throughout this book are those of an experienced supervisor of non-native writers of English. Some supervisors may provide less advice to students before they write the different parts of their dissertation while others may provide more advice, including some of the post-writing feedback areas that are referred to in this book. Finally, it should be realised that the areas covered in both the advice and feedback sections of the book are not intended to be an exhaustive outline of advice or feedback topics. It is hoped that some of the ideas presented in the following chapters will provide guidance for those seeking it.

2

ADVICE AND FEEDBACK IN THE PROVISIONAL ENROLMENT PERIOD

Chapter 2 identifies the pre-writing advice and post-writing feedback that supervisors may consider necessary for their dissertation students during the period of enrolment leading up to their confirmation in the programme of study. The chapter is presented in two parts: Part One refers to the pre-writing advice and Part Two refers to the post-writing feedback.

PART ONE: PRE-WRITING ADVICE

Advice before Enrolment

Students seeking enrolment at my university and supervision with me as their primary supervisor will typically signal their wishes in an email. Most often a proposal is attached together with a CV and supporting documentation such as qualification transcripts. However, on some occasions, this additional material is not included or it is lacking in the detail that is needed for making a judgement call on whether or not to accept the applicant. Although applicants typically identify the broad area of research interest, they may have only had limited access to up-to-date literature, so they will often be given (a) advice about what books and articles to consult (see Box 2.1 for typical titles recommended) and (b) ideas about how they can access this material so that they can resubmit as detailed a proposal as possible. That said, I learned early on in my career that while brief and explicit direction is appropriate, nothing more than this should be offered because there is no guarantee that the student will finally be offered a place or will actually accept an offer of a place at the university.

BOX 2.1 SOME BOOK TITLE RECOMMENDATIONS

Area of focus	Recommended titles
Methodology	Mackey, A., & Gass, S. (2005). *Second language research: Methodology and design.* London: Lawrence Erlbaum Associates. Cresswell, J. (2009). *Research design: Qualitative, quantitative and mixed methods approaches.* London: Sage. Dornyei, Z. (2007). *Research methods in Applied Linguistics: Quantitative, qualitative and mixed methodologies.* Oxford: Oxford University Press.
Second language acquisition theories	Mitchell, R., Myles, R., & Marsden, E. (1998). *Second language learning theories.* London: Routledge. Ortega, L. (2009). *Understanding second language acquisition.* London: Hodder Education.
Written corrective feedback	Bitchener, J., & Ferris, D. (2012). *Written corrective feedback in second language acquisition and writing.* New York: Routledge. Bitchener, J., & Storch, N. (2016). *Written corrective feedback for L2 development.* Bristol: Multilingual Matters.
Thesis and dissertation writing	Bitchener, J. (2010). *Writing an Applied Linguistics thesis or dissertation: A guide to presenting empirical research.* Houndsmill, UK: Palgrave Macmillan. Cooley, L., & Lewkowicz, J. (2003). *Dissertation writing in practice: Turning ideas into text.* Hong Kong: Hong Kong University Press.

Another area of advice that may often be given to students before enrolment is the extent to which they have yet to pitch the proposal at an appropriate level. For instance, it may not signal the original contribution the research is expected to make to the field or it may be that further consideration needs to be given to other aspects of the proposal before a decision can be made to supervise the student (e.g. accuracy and coherence; clarity about the relationship between aims or research questions and methodology and design, especially sources/methods of data collection relevant to the areas of focus).

Advice before the Confirmation of Candidature

Advice during the first 6–9 months covers a wide range of topics and is very much related to a sequence of discussions and advice given in the very first meeting with a new student. The sequence that works well for me and my students is outlined in this section.

The Focus and Expectations of Doctoral Study

In the first meeting with new students, I try to find out what understandings they have of differences between Masters and doctoral study. Typically, they have not really thought too much about this, apart from realising that the dissertation is a bigger piece of research and therefore involves the writing of a bigger document. Thus, a part of the first meeting includes a discussion of the university's profile of a doctoral graduate (presented in Box 2.2). Attention is drawn to what doctoral graduates are expected to know and be able to do once they have completed their studies. Highlighted in the discussion is the need for students to become more and more independent of their supervisor during the supervision period. To help students move in this direction I require students themselves to try first to answer any questions they have during the supervision process. My role then is to confirm their answers or guide them to a consideration of other possibilities. Each university will have a document that is similar to this on their website or in school/departmental handbooks (or equivalent).

BOX 2.2 PROFILE OF A DOCTORAL GRADUATE

A doctoral graduate is expected to have:

- Advanced specialist/discipline knowledge that makes an original contribution to a particular field of enquiry and as appropriate to local and global communities;
- A mastery of a body of knowledge, including a high level of understanding of conceptual and theoretical elements, in a field of study;
- A high level of understanding and appreciation of the philosophical basis, methodologies and characteristics of scholarship, research and creative work in their field of study;
- An advanced ability to analyse information where relevant, using appropriate tools, technologies and methods;
- An advanced capacity for critical appraisal of relevant scholarly literature/knowledge;
- An advanced ability to initiate, design, conduct, sustain and report research;

- Personal, professional, intellectual integrity, respect, and understanding of the ethical dimensions of research and scholarly activity and where appropriate demonstrate understanding the principles in practice of the Treaty of Waitangi (settlement treaty between Maori and Pakeha New Zealanders in 1840);
- A critical understanding and appreciation of the acquisition of knowledge and professional learning for work practice;
- Significant expertise through the research, practice/work, leadership or management roles in their field of study;
- An advanced capacity to communicate ideas effectively to a range of audiences inside the field of study or discipline and to the wider community;
- Confidence and knowledge to make critical commentary on relevant and topical issues in their field of study.

Expectations of the Student and the Supervisor

Second, I explain the role of the key personnel the students will interact with during their years of study, including the supervision team members (academic or faculty members and allied/support members). In particular, this leads to a discussion about (a) my role as their primary supervisor, (b) my expectations and ways of operating and (c) my expectations of them as students. This discussion centres around the university's Code of Practice for Supervisors. The document covers the general, administrative and academic responsibilities of a supervisor as well as the responsibilities of students (see Appendix B). This is followed by a discussion of the supervisor–student agreement. While it specifies the areas that should be included in an agreement between both parties (see Box 2.3), it provides options for both parties to include or not include, as well as space for anything else that is discussed. The agreement can be revised from time to time if either party wants an amendment.

BOX 2.3 OUTLINE OF KEY AREAS FOR CONSIDERATION IN THE SUPERVISOR– STUDENT AGREEMENT

- Schedule of first three meetings
- Meetings and communication strategies
- Supervisory advice and support, including feedback
- Time management

(Continued)

12 Advice/Feedback in Provisional Enrolment Period

(Continued)

- Roles of the supervisory team and others
- Meetings
- Records, minutes, emails
- Resolving disagreements/conflict
- Monitoring progress
- Resources provided by the university
- Assessment and examination
- Extensions and deferments
- The research project and ethical issues
- Intellectual property
- Conflicts of interest

Key Stages in the Doctoral Journey

Third, I explain the key stages of the doctoral journey as outlined in Box 2.4. The key stages are listed in the order in which they are to be completed. Before any of these stages are started, students are required to have a meeting with the supervisor to discuss what will be done and how it will be done. Having this discussion (during which advice is provided about what is expected) minimises the number of iterations as well as the amount of time that supervisors have to spend on reading the drafts and providing feedback. The first full draft is often the culmination of several meetings and feedback on sections within the application proposal. The date of submission is recorded in the first column. The second column may be expanded if more than one section needs to be revised. The third column records the date when a revision of the first full draft has been submitted. The fourth column records the date when the supervisor has signed off on the area, indicating that s/he does not need to see it again.

BOX 2.4   KEY STAGES IN THE RESEARCH AND WRITING OF A DISSERTATION

	Full draft 1	*Section revisions*	*Full draft 2*	*Final draft*
Pre-proposal outline				
Preparation of PGR9 proposal: literature review				
Preparation of PGR9 proposal: methodology				

Preparation of PowerPoint presentation				
Presentation of PowerPoint presentation				
Literature review chapter				
Methodology chapter				
Preparation of ethics application				
Submission of ethics application				
Introduction chapter – first full version				
Pilot study – design				
Pilot study – conduct				
Pilot study – report/chapter				
Methodology chapter revisions post pilot study				
Main study – data collection				
Main study – data analysis				
Results chapter				
Revise introduction, literature and methodology chapters in light of results				
Discussion chapter				
Conclusion chapter				
Revise Introduction in light of Conclusion				
Abstract				
Front and end matter				
Complete thesis checklist				
Submit 3 spiral bound copies				

The Focus and Timing of Each Stage

The pre-proposal outline is described below as part of the initial action plan.

- The PGR9 proposal is the confirmation proposal that students submit to the Doctoral Board when seeking confirmation of candidature. The two key sections of the proposal are the literature review and the methodology/design of the proposed investigation. As well as presenting the proposal document to the Doctoral Board, students also present a 20-minute presentation of their proposal (in the form of a PowerPoint presentation) and

14 Advice/Feedback in Provisional Enrolment Period

answer questions from Board members and the general audience for 10 minutes after the presentation.

- The first full drafts of the literature and methodology chapters are then completed so students are less likely to find that they have ignored something important once the ethics application and pilot study have been started.
- The ethics application is written next. While the students are waiting for approval from the university's ethics committee, they complete the first full draft of their introduction chapter. Doing this at this stage means the literature and methodology content is still fresh in their minds and they are more likely to provide a clear introduction to their work than if they leave it until a later stage in their journey.
- Once the pilot study has been completed, students write a report and make any necessary revisions to their methodology chapter.
- At this stage, they are ready to conduct their main study. While they are collecting data and analysing it, they update these two sections in their methodology chapter. Usually this involves the addition of steps or processes that were not identified before starting these stages.
- The results chapter is written as the data are analysed.
- Once the results are clear, any revisions, in light of the pilot study findings, to the introduction, literature and methodology chapters are completed.
- While a return to these chapters is fresh in the students' minds, they work on their discussion of results chapter and then the conclusion chapter.
- Any revisions are then made to the introduction chapter that may be considered necessary in light of what has been presented in the conclusion chapter.
- The abstract is then written before front and end matter are assembled.

I find it is useful to have a discussion about these stages early on so that expectations about what needs to happen and the sequence in which they occur are understood and don't come as a surprise to the student. While the overall sequence of stages is standard for all students, the timing of each activity may vary from student to student. Because the key stages document is frequently referred to during the three or four years of the programme of study, I spend more time in the first meeting focusing on what is involved in the provisional year. This includes a discussion of what is involved in preparing the confirmation proposal (discussed below) – a task that students typically work on for about 8–9 months. At this stage, the discussion is more of an introductory overview of what is required in the proposal than an in-depth discussion of its component parts. More detail is provided as part of the advice that is given to students before they start a new aspect of their work. Before the confirmation proposal is considered further, two preliminary steps are discussed: a consideration of the original proposal and an initial action plan.

The Original Research Proposal

The second meeting with new students focuses on their research proposal. I begin this meeting with a discussion of the proposal they submitted when they applied for enrolment in the doctoral programme. I like to find out, first of all, how committed they are to the focus of the proposal because sometimes they may have changed their mind as a result of further reading and thinking. For instance, some students may want to change part of the proposal while others may want to make a more substantial change that will require them to undertake a more extensive reading programme. The discussion about their original proposal is also important because it provides the first chance for me to tell them exactly what I think about their proposal (e.g. about its intended direction, scope and feasibility). The potential theoretical, empirical and methodological contribution to the field of knowledge is also an important part of this discussion because I want to be sure that the study is going to have every chance (a) of making an original contribution and (b) of being pitched at the level expected for a doctoral degree.

The Initial Action Plan

Once I am satisfied that the proposal is worth confirming and that the student is committed to its focus, an action plan for the upcoming weeks is decided upon. This plan includes a period of reading and thinking that is negotiated with the student and that ends with a series of answers to the following questionnaire in Box 2.5. The number of recommended sentences and paragraphs are only indicative. Depending on the number of changes and the breadth and depth of reading already completed, students may take anything between a few weeks or a few months to complete the questions.

BOX 2.5 PROPOSAL QUESTIONNAIRE

1 What is the problem or issue that you want to investigate and why is it a problem? (one paragraph of 5–6 sentences)
2 What literature (theoretical, empirical and methodological) underpins the problem or issue? (2 paragraphs of 5–6 sentences)
3 What gaps are there in the literature (theoretical, empirical and methodological)? (1 paragraph of 5–6 sentences)
4 Why is/are the gap(s) worth investigating? (1 paragraph of 5–6 sentences)
5 What do you think your research questions might be? (list these)
6 What research approach and methods do you think you would find useful and why? (2–3 paragraphs of 5–6 sentences)
7 Provide a bibliography of your reading.

---

16 Advice/Feedback in Provisional Enrolment Period

Once students have submitted their answers, a further discussion is scheduled and any further necessary amendments are identified.

Approaches and Strategies for Writing the Confirmation Proposal

I explain to the students that once they have made any necessary amendments, their next task will be to extend their reading where necessary and provide a first draft of the confirmation proposal. The key elements of the proposal are outlined in Box 2.6.

BOX 2.6 KEY ELEMENTS OF THE CONFIRMATION PROPOSAL

1 Background information about the applicant
2 Topic and research questions
3 Rationale and significance of the study
4 Literature background relevant to the focus of the proposed research
5 Methodology and design of the proposed research
6 Expected timeline

During their reading programme, students often spend so much time on the theoretical and empirical literature that they forget about the methodological literature. I draw their attention to this so that they read and think about each of these aspects from the very beginning.

In the following section, I outline the advice that students are given on the writing of the literature review component of the confirmation proposal.

The Literature Review Component of the Confirmation Proposal

Before students decide upon their further reading programme, it is useful to find out what they know about conducting a focused and comprehensive review of the literature (theoretical, empirical and methodological). This discussion may take place before they complete the proposal questionnaire presented earlier. However, more often than not, this discussion will take place after the questionnaire answers have been discussed as I am more likely to have a clearer idea of their needs for advice. I have found over the years that it is unwise to simply assume that they know what to do and that they know how to go about doing it in the most effective and timely manner.

Typically, I find that students have a general understanding of what is involved but that they sometimes go about the task without a mind to the future, that is, without a consideration about how they will eventually use the knowledge they have gained from their further reading when writing the proposal. Thinking about the relevance of the literature to the problem, issue or research questions at the centre of their proposed study and about how the selected literature will be organised to present a case or argument are two considerations that are sometimes not fully understood. Thus, I discuss with them a series of approaches or strategies that my students, over the years, have found helpful. I stress the importance of being organised and the need to think carefully and critically as they read each new text, not only about what each text is saying but also about the relationship between what the various texts are saying. I explain that the writing of a relevant and focused proposal begins with the quality of their reading and thinking during the reading programme. The key pieces of advice that I provide include the need to: (a) keep a record of the focus/foci of each piece of literature; (b) create a mind-map to show the relationship between topics/headings identified in the literature; (c) scope the macro structure of the argument using a table of contents and/or PowerPoint slides; and (d) write an argument overview.

Keeping a Record of the Focus or Foci of Each Piece of Literature

I explain that a spreadsheet can be used to record key information about each piece of literature. Table 2.1 illustrates what part of a spreadsheet may look like. Brevity of record is essential in this type of record. If students want to record additional information for later reference, they can do so in other files. In column one, a list of key areas considered to be important and typically referred to in journal articles and book chapters reporting on theory and research are identified. Brief notes (e.g. key words or headings) about each of these areas can be recorded in column two and in following columns as illustrated in reference to Bitchener (2012). Students may wish to add other areas to this list. The value of this type of record is that it (a) enables students to see similarities and differences at a glance and (b) provides them with a concise overview of the literature. Some students also like to record elsewhere other details about the literature (e.g. definitions of constructs and terms, key quotes and cross references to other literature).

Creating a Mind-map to Show the Relationship(s) Between Literature Topics/Headings

From the Bitchener (2012) entry in Table 2.1, key topics or themes can be identified and recorded. These can then be included in a mind-map as the

18 Advice/Feedback in Provisional Enrolment Period

TABLE 2.1 Key Information on Each Piece of Literature

	Bitchener (2012)	*Additional authors*
Key topics or themes	Acquired vs learned competence Implicit vs explicit knowledge Procedural vs declarative knowledge Explicit/implicit conversion debate	
Key theories	Skill development theories (Anderson; McLaughlin) Noticing with awareness vs understanding	
Research questions	Are some types of written CF more effective than others for L2 development?	
Methodology & Design	Pre-test/treatment/post-test 4 groups (3 treatment and 1 control) Linguistic focus: articles, simple past tense; prepositions	
Context & participants	ESL learners (mixed L1) 75 low intermediate level	
Data sources	3 writing tasks Same genre	
Data analysis	Error analysis ANOVA testing of effectiveness of different groups	
Key findings	Direct error correction plus oral and written meta-linguistic explanation is more effective than direct error correction alone for articles and past simple tense	
Limitations	Linguistic categories do not distinguish between sub-categories Treatment groups sometimes have more than one type of written CF type	

reading and thinking progresses and be moved about on the mind-map as new relationships between topics are understood during the process. Box 2.7 shows what one section of such a mind-map might include.

Thinking about relationships in this way means that students can start to focus on which topics/headings will be included in their proposal argument and about the order in which the topics/headings will be included so that their argument(s) is(are) as logical and cohesive as possible. This approach means that the 'brain work' is done 'en route' rather than being left to a later stage in the reading process when some of the text detail may have been forgotten. Mind-maps can become cluttered over time so separate mind-maps can then be created for certain topics/headings that need to be expanded. During the reading process, some initial headings may be subdivided into two or more additional headings while others may be collapsed into fewer headings. As Box 2.7 illustrates, arrows can be used to show the relationship between topics/headings. Horizontal arrows can be used to signal whether a certain topic would make logical sense if

Advice/Feedback in Provisional Enrolment Period 19

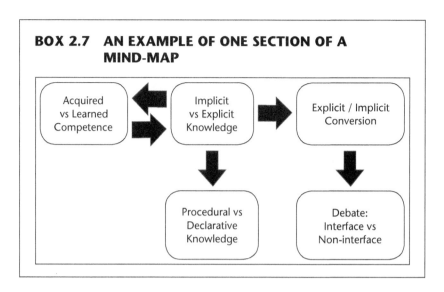

BOX 2.7   AN EXAMPLE OF ONE SECTION OF A MIND-MAP

it were to be discussed before a certain other topic (e.g. in reference to Box 2.7, implicit vs explicit knowledge before explicit/implicit conversion). Sometimes, it may not matter which of two topics/headings is discussed first. In this case, horizontal arrows pointing in both directions can be used to signal this possibility (e.g. in reference to Box 2.7, acquired vs learned competence or implicit vs explicit knowledge). On other occasions, students may want to create a new heading to signal that a topic needs to be expanded into a number of parts. For example, this may occur if there are several ways of defining a construct or term. This expansion of ideas/headings might be placed under the original topic/heading with vertical arrows signalling the relationship (e.g. in reference to Box 2.7, procedural vs declarative knowledge).

Scoping the Macro Structure of the Argument Using a Table of Contents and/or PowerPoint Slides

Creating a table of contents from mind-map relationships can help students to create a skeletal outline of the macro structure of their argument. As this is created, it is easy to see where the argument is heading and whether or not there are irrelevant topics or gaps in the argument. It can also reveal more easily whether certain topics or units need to be moved to a different position in the macro argument. An example of what a table of contents might look like is shown in Box 2.8.

20 Advice/Feedback in Provisional Enrolment Period

BOX 2.8   AN EXAMPLE OF A TABLE OF CONTENTS FOR ONE KEY HEADING

1.0   Goal of L2 learning: native/near-native competence
    1.1   Two types of competence: learned and acquired
2.0   Two types of knowledge: explicit and implicit
    2.1   Relationship between knowledge and competence types
    2.2   Explicit–implicit conversion debate
        2.2.1   Interface position vs. non-interface position
3.0   Explicit information processing
    3.1   Skill acquisition theories
        3.1.1   Anderson
        3.1.2   McLaughlin
        3.1.3   DeKeyser
    3.2   Information processing stages

Once students have created a table of contents, I ask them to talk me through the argument of the table of contents. This step reveals the extent to which they understand the relationship between the ideas represented by the various headings and sub-headings. For students who experience some difficulty with this task, I recommend that they develop their table of contents more fully by creating PowerPoint slides (one for each major heading). Box 2.9 is an example of a slide which provides more information about one sub-section of a student's dissertation on the cognitive processing of new information about a target language, namely, motivational and situational factors that may have a moderating effect on how second language learners cognitively process new linguistic information.

BOX 2.9   AN EXAMPLE OF A POWERPOINT SLIDE ON ONE SUB-HEADING

Motivational and Situational Factors that May Account for Incomplete Cognitive Processing

1   *Motivational variables*

- Frequent and fluctuating desire to engage in writing activities that focus on accuracy
- Attitudes and beliefs about different types of feedback
- Attitudes and beliefs about revising

2   *Situational variables*

- Time of day
- Student–teacher and student–student relationships

This process of providing more information about each heading/topic can help students see the relationship between topics/headings more clearly and enable them to articulate the argument more effectively when they are asked to explain it and write about it. This slide identifies some of the motivational and situational variables that a student had in mind when suggesting that these factors may have a moderating effect. If the supervisor is not told what the factors are, there may be no way of knowing whether the selection of factors is valid and relevant to the wider argument outlined in a table of contents.

Writing an Argument Overview

This strategy asks the student to use the table of contents and/or the PowerPoint slides to write an argument overview (c.300–350 words) for a major section of a chapter. Having completed a table of contents and/or PowerPoint slides, most students are able to create a reasonable first draft of the argument. Some students find it helpful if sample overviews are read and discussed first. The argument in Box 2.10 (about the theoretical justification of one research question in a dissertation) illustrates the type of overview that might be expected for one unit or section of the review. A deconstruction and discussion of this overview can also help students see how they can signal the relationship between the various components of the argument. The key points that I draw students' attention to include the following:

1   Each of the ten propositions in Box 2.10 refers to a key idea of the overall argument of one major section of the literature review and each of these propositions can be used to determine the wording of the topic sentence that will introduce a development of the idea.
2   I ask students to decide on a heading (ten words maximum) for each of the ten propositions so these can be used as sub-headings. For example, the heading of proposition 1 might be: Theoretical case for cognitive processing of written CF (8 words). The heading for proposition 2 might be: The central goal of L2 learning (6 words). The heading for proposition 3 might be: Knowledge bases of acquired and learned competence (7 words). These three examples could be referred to as an example of what supervisors might ask students to do with the other seven propositions.
3   I draw the students' attention to the relationship between each of the ten propositions so they can see that each proposition leads logically and explicitly to the next proposition. In doing so, I refer to some of the key words in each proposition (including in some cases the use of discourse markers) that facilitate the cohesive relationship between ideas. For example, I explain that proposition 1 outlines the aim of the section of the review and that proposition 2 explains how the section will begin. Proposition 3 then explains how the author of the section refers to the role of the different

22 Advice/Feedback in Provisional Enrolment Period

knowledge bases (implicit and explicit knowledge) in the learned competence of a student and how this can lead to acquired competence. The argument throughout the overview is framed with meta-text where the author tells the reader what s/he is going to do. For example, having stated the overall aim of the section in proposition 1, the author, in proposition 2, uses the words 'I begin by explaining…' and follows this, in proposition 3, with the words 'In doing so…', thereby signalling how the focus of proposition 3 will be a development of what has been introduced in proposition 2. It should also be noted that both the active and passive voices have been used in the overview. Supervisors may prefer only one or the other being used rather than a mix of the two. Having discussed these points with students, supervisors may ask students to continue the line of explanation for the other propositions. Finally, it should be pointed out to students that they need to choose key words carefully. For example, it is useful to draw their attention to key verbs (e.g. 'present', 'draw upon', 'explain', 'argue', 'describe' and 'acknowledge') as they signal exactly what the author plans to do or cover in each sub-section.

BOX 2.10   AN EXAMPLE OF AN ARGUMENT OVERVIEW

1   The aim of this section is to present a case that supports a role for written corrective feedback (CF) in L2 development, drawing upon theoretical perspectives that have something to say about the cognitive processing of L2 information and the potential of written CF as explicit L2 input to facilitate such processing.

2   I begin by explaining that the central goal of L2 learning is the acquisition of native or near-native speaker competence.

3   In doing so, I argue that acquired competence which draws upon implicit knowledge can be developed from learned competence that draws upon explicit knowledge such as that provided by written CF.

4   Explaining this process, I refer to the skill acquisition models of Anderson and McLaughlin to show how explicit, declarative L2 knowledge can be proceduralised through meaningful, contextualised practice over time to a point where it may be converted to implicit, acquired knowledge.

5   Then, I describe the specific information processing stages that have been identified by cognitive theorists like Tomlin and Villa, Schmidt and Swain, for example, and that have been represented in frameworks such as the one designed by Gass (1997).

6 In processing written CF as input, Gass' framework explains that learners need to attend to written CF as input if they are to progress through the other stages that will enable them to produce modified accurate output and on-going accurate output in new written texts over time.

7 The other stages include an understanding (comprehended input), an internalisation and an integration of written CF as input.

8 Producing accurate output as a result of this conscious processing is the beginning of a longer consolidation process during which practice is believed to facilitate acquired competence.

9 I acknowledge the possibility that this linear route towards acquisition may be both facilitated and interrupted as a result of the type of written CF a learner is provided with and as a result of intervening individual internal (cognitive and motivational/affective) factors and individual external factors.

10 The extent to which these theoretical proposals are valid explanations of the acquisition route is something that only empirical research can investigate. This will be the focus of the next section.

The Methodology/Design Component of the Confirmation Proposal

The six steps identified in Box 2.11 can be followed when students prepare this section of their confirmation proposal. Step 1 will include, for example, the methodological approach, the design of the study, data sources, the methods/procedures of data collection and data analysis, trustworthiness or reliability and validity, and ethical issues. This listing might also include the pilot study, particularly if it differs from the main study in any major respects. It is important to discuss the key sections with the supervisor before writing commences in order to reduce the amount of feedback that may be necessary if this step is not included. Step 3 might be included within step 1 as part of the reading programme. Supervisors may need to guide their students with a selection of dissertations that are relevant to the focus of their own students' proposals. Step 4 is intended to be a development of the initial table of contents. Discussing these with the supervisor before writing commences will enable any gaps or irrelevant content to be easily identified. Step 6 may focus on the writing of one or two sub-sections first and be followed by a discussion with the supervisor about the approach that has been taken. It is pointed out elsewhere in this book that students' first drafts are often strong in description but lacking in justification, so checking one or two sections first may be useful to establish the expected focus of the write-up.

24 Advice/Feedback in Provisional Enrolment Period

BOX 2.11 STEPS IN THE PREPARATION OF THE METHODOLOGY/DESIGN COMPONENT

1 Based on your reading, design a table of contents or list the key topics that the methodology will include
2 Discuss the table of contents with the supervisor
3 Consult other relevant dissertations and confirmation proposals to see what they include
4 Compile a list of key points or bullet points for each topic or heading of the methodology (in the form of PowerPoint slides, with one slide per topic/heading)
5 Discuss these bullet points with the supervisor to identify any obvious gaps
6 Write up the methodology/design section of the proposal

The Rationale and Significance Components of the Confirmation Proposal

The three steps identified in Box 2.12 can be followed when students prepare this section of the confirmation proposal. Step I has proven to be essential with most students because, if a discussion of what is expected with regard to each of these aspects is not part of the initial elicitation and advice session before students start writing this section, they can very easily not differentiate between the two and can often over-emphasise one of the two aspects.

BOX 2.12 STEPS IN THE PREPARATION OF RATIONALE AND SIGNIFICANCE SECTIONS OF THE CONFIRMATION PROPOSAL

1 Discuss with students the meaning of the terms 'rationale' and 'significance' to ensure they have the same understanding that you have about what is expected when each of these components are discussed
2 Create a bullet point list of key reasons (rationale) the research was important enough to have been proposed
3 Create a bullet point list of key predictions about the expected significance of the research, including a consideration that justifies the predictions and reveals who will benefit from the research and in what way(s)

Advice/Feedback in Provisional Enrolment Period **25**

In Box 2.13, an example of a good rationale and significant statement is presented even though it is a little repetitive in places. The statement begins in paragraphs 1 and 2 with a personal reason or motivation for the area of research and proceeds in paragraphs 3 to 5 with an outline of the rationale or reasons for proposing the investigation. Paragraph 5 bring together a statement about the literature gaps and, as a result, a statement about the aims or purposes of the proposed study. Paragraph 6 continues with a statement about the focus of the study and begins a discussion of the contribution or significance of the study that extends across the remaining paragraphs. In terms of the contribution of the study, it would also have been good to read what the student thinks the contribution might be to the development of methodology for further research in the area. A clearer distinction between the theoretical and empirical contributions of the study could also have been provided. While these additional features are often not fully realised at the proposal stage, they do tend to be identified once further reading has been engaged with as students consider the first full draft of their introduction and literature review chapters. The example in Box 2.13 could be used by supervisors as they discuss their expectations.

BOX 2.13 EXAMPLE OF A RATIONALE AND SIGNIFICANCE STATEMENT

Paragraph 1

As an English teacher of 10 years, I have taught English to students of both instructional settings: EFL (Iran) and ESL (New Zealand). In my cooperation with ESL teachers in Australia and New Zealand, and in my limited teaching experience within the ESL context, I was surprised to see differences in how EFL and ESL teachers approach learners' errors. In trying to find the reason for the differences, I observed both EFL and ESL classrooms over the last couple of years. I also had discussions with the teachers on how they viewed error correction in general. Most Iranian teachers I spoke to believed that it is important to correct errors in a way that learners notice it – explicit correction. On the other hand, some of the ESL teachers told me they believe fluency to be more important than accuracy and even though they believe error correction to be necessary, they mostly choose delayed rather than immediate feedback so as to not interrupt the flow of the communication.

Paragraph 2

My personal experience with the obvious differences between EFL and ESL teachers' error correction techniques raised many questions which became

(Continued)

(Continued)

the basis of this PhD research proposal. I chose to investigate and compare teacher feedback, and in particular interactional feedback (hereafter IF), in the two contexts in detail.

Paragraph 3

While there is much research in the literature on how various classroom aspects compare across different settings, there is scope for in-depth investigations into differences in how EFL and ESL teachers use IF in their classrooms. It is generally assumed that teachers' beliefs provide a basis for action (Borg, 2011), and the decisions they make in classrooms can be affected by their beliefs (Arnett & Turnbull, 2008). It is therefore important to initially investigate teachers' beliefs on IF to see how they drive classroom behaviour.

Paragraph 4

There have been calls for further investigation into teacher cognition by scholars (e.g. Borg, 2003; Mori, 2011) that state the importance of investigating what teachers think, know and believe, and the relationship of these mental constructs to what teachers do in the language teaching classrooms. In addition, Basturkmen et al. (2004) and Basturkmen (2012) have pointed to the lack of research that investigates the mismatch between teacher beliefs and classroom practices, and the possible factors underlying such mismatches. This study is therefore intended to take up these scholars' calls for investigation.

Paragraph 5

Thus, this research project is intended to fill this gap in the literature by providing a fine-grained investigation into what language teachers (a) think about, and (b) how they practice IF. In particular, the purpose of this study is three-fold: (1) to investigate Iranian EFL and New Zealand ESL teachers' beliefs about IF and their actual classroom practices to see if there is any kind of mismatch between beliefs and practices; (2) to determine how similar/different the EFL and ESL teachers are with regard to teacher cognition on IF and its practice; and (3) if there is a mismatch between teachers' beliefs and practices, to determine what factor(s) cause such mismatches.

Paragraph 6

The focus of this study is rather unique as it aims to examine teachers' side of the story about IF, an area which has not received attention in

SLA research. As a result, the picture of IF will be broadened. It is safe to claim that no research has yet compared teachers' beliefs and their actual classroom practices about IF in the two instructional settings of EFL and ESL. This study will therefore be first to investigate similarities/differences between Iran's EFL and New Zealand's ESL contexts from a teacher cognition point of view.

Paragraph 7

Due to the qualitative approach of this research and the in-depth investigation into EFL and ESL teachers' inner worlds, the study will provide valuable insight for other researchers and teachers by providing a broader picture of how beliefs may affect classroom behaviour. The results of this research will shed light on this area of second/foreign language learning, and as a result will benefit English language teachers of both contexts (ESL and EFL). It is expected that the results obtained will contribute to a better understanding of what beliefs language teachers hold on IF and how they interact with learners. This line of research is crucial, as teachers' roles as active thinkers are being recognised more than ever. The more teachers are aware of the effect their beliefs may have on their corrective behaviour, the better equipped they will be to approach students with techniques that can enhance learning, in addition to making learners' errors work for them.

Paragraph 8

In terms of pedagogical implications, given the importance of providing learners with effective feedback on their ill-formed language, being aware of common teacher beliefs on IF enables teachers to support learners more effectively in their efforts to achieve L2 acquisition. Also, this study can further underscore the central role teachers play in language classrooms, and can ultimately lead to teacher educators contributing more to the development of quality amongst teachers. Ultimately, as the current study attempts to determine if a mismatch between teachers' beliefs and practices exists, it can help English teachers become aware of the possible inconsistencies and adjust their error correction techniques accordingly. As the existing literature in this regard is insufficient, teachers may simply not be aware that what they think might not always translate into how they behave. Therefore, the results of this study can benefit teachers, and in particular, language teachers in opening their eyes to potential mismatches in their beliefs and practices.

(Continued)

28 Advice/Feedback in Provisional Enrolment Period

(Continued)

Paragraph 9

This study can consequently be significant to English teachers of both EFL and ESL contexts, as it attempts to determine how their perceptions and beliefs may affect their actual classroom practices. Similarly, it will be fruitful to researchers who want to study in similar areas of teacher cognition and the relationship between beliefs and practices. As a teacher, what I will learn from this investigation will have an influence on how I interact with my students, how I provide effective feedback, and how I discuss my teaching approaches and corrective feedback techniques with colleagues.

Once these key sections of the confirmation proposal have been completed, students can prepare for the oral presentation of their proposal. Typically, the presentation will be for 20 minutes (i.e. like a conference presentation) with 10 minutes given to questions at the end. During the question and answer session, students may be required to defend, explain more or clarify any part of their presentation.

Writing the Oral PowerPoint Presentation of the Confirmation Proposal

Box 2.14 provides students with an outline of the type of content that can be presented in their slides. The number of slides is indicative only. Some of the slides may be eliminated if two or more are reduced to just one slide, for example. Appendix C provides an example of the slides that one doctoral student included in her oral presentation.

BOX 2.14 OVERVIEW OF SLIDES FOR AN ORAL PRESENTATION OF THE CONFIRMATION PROPOSAL

Number of slides	Focus of slides
1	State the title
1	Provide an overview of presentation
1–2	State the key research questions/hypotheses
1–2	Define key terms and constructs used in the title and research questions/hypotheses
2–3	Explain the rationale (key reasons) for undertaking the research

1–2	Identify the significance (expected contribution) of the research
5–6	Review the literature: key theoretical frameworks and published research, including what is known and not known (gaps)
1	Provide a summary table pairing up gaps and research questions/hypotheses
1	Explain the philosophical perspective informing the research approach
1–2	Outline the methodological approach (e.g. mixed methods; quantitative; qualitative) and state the rationale for each approach
1	Provide a table that matches each research question with the relevant data sources
1–2	Identify data collection processes (context, participants, procedures)
1–2	Describe the data analysis process
1	Explain the validity and reliability (trustworthiness) measures
1	Identify the key ethical issues to be addressed
1	Provide a timetable for completion
1	Identify key references

When the slides have been designed, students should do a mock run of their presentation. There are a number of reasons for suggesting that this be done. First, it may be the first PowerPoint presentation students have done. As a result, they are likely to run over the 20 minutes allocated so will need to consider ways in which they can reduce the amount of content they plan to present. It may be that they spend too much time elaborating on a particular point on a slide or it may be that some of the slide detail could be reduced and referred to in the question and answer session if necessary. Second, students sometimes don't realise that they may have a limited understanding of a certain aspect of their presentation. Presenting such material will signal to the supervisor (and other students) whether or not they are able to explain their points clearly and whether or not they are able to explicitly articulate the line of argument running through the points on a slide or across several slides. In my context, the mock run is typically done at cohort/pot luck meetings (described earlier) as it provides a good opportunity for other students to comment on what they thought was effective and what was not effective about the presentation. Thus, it becomes a valuable learning experience for them too, especially if they have yet to present their confirmation proposal.

30 Advice/Feedback in Provisional Enrolment Period

PART TWO: POST-WRITING FEEDBACK

Despite the pre-writing advice that students may be given, post-writing feedback will always be necessary. This is understandable because the application of new knowledge (such as that which is provided as pre-writing advice) requires a range of skills that some students take longer to acquire than others. Thus, the range and depth of feedback will typically vary from student to student. The type of feedback that each student requires can depend, to a large extent, on their earlier academic writing experience (at both undergraduate and graduate levels) and on the extent to which they developed new knowledge and skills during those years of study. This section identifies some of the areas in which post-writing feedback may be needed during the pre-confirmation period of enrolment: (a) feedback before enrolment; (b) feedback on the initial proposal; (c) feedback on the confirmation proposal; (d) feedback on the slides for the oral presentation of the proposal; and (e) feedback on the PowerPoint slides for the oral presentation.

Feedback before Enrolment

As I explained earlier, feedback before enrolment should be kept to a minimum because the applicant may not accept an offer of a place in the programme of study. There is growing anecdotal evidence that some students exploit the generosity of supervisors known in the field when they have no intention of studying at the supervisor's university. Consequently, the type of feedback I give on an initial proposal is little more than that which suggests where students should provide more detail in their proposal or where they need to pitch the proposal at a higher level.

Feedback on the Initial Proposal

There are five areas of the initial proposal that often require some degree of feedback: (a) its focus; (b) the accuracy and completeness of the proposal's content; (c) the importance of the intended area of focus; (d) the feasibility of the proposed research; and (e) the level of originality of the project.

The Focus of the Proposal

In the early stages of developing a proposal, there can be a tendency for some students to want to offer an investigation into what should really be seen as a life's work. The scope, as revealed by a statement of aims or as an outline of proposed research questions, may sometimes be too broad, so feedback will be needed to help students limit the gaps they have identified in the literature when designing their research questions/hypotheses. Once this has been done, the research questions/hypotheses may then need to be redrafted. It is not uncommon for students to include too many issues or factors in a single research question/hypothesis. Some direction on how to break up questions into those that focus on only one issue rather than on two or more issues may be required. Sometimes, key terms or constructs in the wording of a research question/hypothesis will need to be more clearly and narrowly defined so that the question/hypothesis can be operationalised. These are some of the issues that may need to be overcome to make sure the questions/hypothesis are clear and manageable. If we consider the research questions (in Box 2.15) that one doctoral applicant presented in her initial proposal, we can see the type of feedback that was given to the applicant.

BOX 2.15   FEEDBACK GIVEN ON RESEARCH QUESTIONS IN AN INITIAL PROPOSAL

Initial research questions	Feedback given on each research question
What is the mediating role of learners' motivation on their reception of written corrective feedback (CF) and to what extent does the level of learners' motivation change during the cognitive processing of written CF?	This question is really two different questions. What aspects of the motivation construct are you planning to investigate? What is meant by 'level' of motivation? You will need to provide some operational questions for each of these two questions so it is clear what you mean by and how you will investigate key words/constructs like: mediate, motivation, reception, level of motivation, cognitive processing.
What are learners' opinions about error correction and different written CF techniques in terms of direct, indirect and meta-linguistic explanation, and is there any correlation between the learners' attitudes and the learners' motivation?	On what written CF issues/topics are you seeking their opinions? Do you only mean their opinions about the value of the three types of written CF you identify here? The second part of the question introduces a new question. The second question seems to be incomplete. Do you mean an interactional effect between the two variables (attitudes and motivation) on the cognitive processing route and/or modified output?
Does learners' interest towards language learning affect learners' motivation to receive written CF?	How do you define 'interest'? What do you mean by 'receive written CF'? Are you referring to their immediate reaction to or response to the written CF they are given?

32 Advice/Feedback in Provisional Enrolment Period

The Accuracy and Completeness of the Proposal's Content

Feedback on the accuracy and completeness of the content in the initial proposal may be required if students have not read extensively in the area they are referring to. For instance, at the time of writing the proposal, they may have only touched on (1) some of the potentially relevant theoretical perspectives that are relevant to their proposal and (2) some of the published empirical and methodological literature. In some contexts, students may have not had access to some of the important literature and so the focus of the proposal may, as a result, be a bit dated or incomplete and, as a result, not be entirely accurate. Supervisors can either advise students to make use of the new resources available to them upon enrolment to update their reading and/or they can offer more specific advice about some of the areas they want their students to explore. Providing a short list of key books, dissertations and journal articles may be helpful but such a list should not be seen as an alternative to students taking the initiative themselves; it should be a starting point only.

The Importance of the Intended Area of Focus

Initial proposals tend to contain more descriptive detail than justified detail about why the area of focus is worthy of investigation. Students may need advice about some of the ways in which they can justify the need for a particular research topic (i.e. the rationale for the proposal). While most students will know that they need to refer to previously published theoretical and empirical literature to identify gaps in this body of knowledge, many sometimes need advice about referring to gaps in theoretical explanation or shortcomings in the methodologies of published empirical studies. It is generally the case that they need to be encouraged to reflect more broadly and more deeply on the importance of the proposed area of research so that they can produce an argument (including description and justification) that is robust and compelling. More often than not, students at this stage will be satisfied with stating only the more obvious reasons for proposing a particular research focus rather than perhaps thinking about the potential of other areas of focus that the published literature has yet to discuss.

The Feasibility of the Proposed Research

Because students have had limited experience in designing and conducting empirical research, it is not surprising that some may not have thought about all the feasibility factors they need to consider. If, as was stated above, the focus of the research questions/hypotheses is not clear, feasibility issues may be difficult to identify. In order to know whether or not a piece of research will be feasible, students will typically need advice from their supervisors about aspects of the proposed methodology that they know will be problematic. It is very difficult for some students to imagine how they will carry out their research, step by step. Those who can visualise the progression of steps are more likely to be successful in identifying potentially problematic areas. Yet, having done that is no guarantee that students will be able to come up with solutions. This is when the supervisor needs to provide advice. However, this does not mean that supervisors should provide advice on every area that may be problematic. They may want their students to discover such areas during the pilot research process or want them to take the initiative in trying to resolve them. That said, supervisors would be unwise to not alert their students to areas that could significantly affect the overall direction of the research if they can see this might occur as a result of their failing to offer advice.

One approach that can help students think about the practicality or feasibility of their research questions is to ask them to provide one or more questions that reveal how the question will be operationalised. If we consider the question in Box 2.15 about the effect of motivation on learners' receipt/response to written CF, students could break the question up into a number of parts to reveal exactly which aspects of the motivation construct they are interested in. This could then be followed up with an outline of the sources they will draw upon for data (e.g. questionnaire; interview). Both indicators of how the question will be investigated can then be trialled in a pilot study and revised if necessary before the main study's data are collected.

The Level of Originality of the Project

At doctoral level, even more so than at Masters level, the research proposal needs to reveal the extent to which the project is likely to produce original new knowledge for the field of investigation. While most students have little difficulty with identifying what will likely be new empirical findings, they often fail to consider the potential of their research for theory-building or the contribution it may make to advancing methodological approaches that can investigate more deeply and robustly the questions or issues that may hitherto have received only scant attention or those that have been methodologically flawed in some way. Even though these insights will be more evident as the student's project progresses, it is not too early for advice to be given about the importance of reflecting on these areas as they develop their proposal and conduct their research.

Feedback on the Confirmation Proposal

Feedback will inevitably be required on all three key sections of the confirmation proposal: the literature review, the methodology and the rationale/ significance section.

Feedback on the Literature Review

While more extensive post-writing feedback on literature reviews is given in Chapter 4 of this book, it is worth identifying, at this stage, some of the main

34 Advice/Feedback in Provisional Enrolment Period

areas on which supervisors will inevitably need to provide feedback when students have produced their first full iteration of the literature review section of the confirmation proposal. For further explanation and discussion of these areas of concern outlined in Box 2.16, see Chapter 4 (literature review section) and Chapter 5 (argument creation).

BOX 2.16   THE FOCUS OF LITERATURE REVIEW FEEDBACK

- **Coverage** of the literature relevant to the focus of the proposed research, including **completeness** of information
- Clarity and **coherence of the argument** that relates the selected content to the focus of the proposed research
- **Criticality** of the review, including an **assessment/evaluation of all claims made and conclusions** drawn by authors and by oneself
- Creation of a **robust argument** that describes and justifies the propositions that are made and that coherently leads from one proposition to another.
- Identification of a range of gaps in knowledge, including not only empirical gaps but also theoretical and methodological gaps

---

Feedback on the Methodology Section

As for the previous section on literature review feedback, a more detailed coverage of the type of feedback that supervisors may need to give their students on the methodology section of the confirmation proposal can be found in Chapter 4 of this book. Nevertheless, it is worth identifying here in Box 2.17 some of the key areas where feedback is typically required on a first full iteration of the confirmation proposal.

BOX 2.17   THE FOCUS OF METHODOLOGY FEEDBACK

- Some sectional headings may have not been included in the listing of methodology components and therefore the content relevant to such headings is likely to have not been included
- Some sectional headings may have been included but with a coverage that is too sketchy for the reader to understand how some aspects of the methodology are to be conducted
- Some aspects of this section may not conform to disciplinary conventions

Advice/Feedback in Provisional Enrolment Period **35**

Feedback on the Rationale/Significance Section

The same issues identified earlier, in relation to the initial proposal, may also require feedback in the confirmation proposal. In particular, the following areas presented in Box 2.18 are likely candidates for feedback.

BOX 2.18 THE FOCUS OF RATIONALE AND SIGNIFICANCE FEEDBACK

- The **rationale** may not have been considered as fully as it could have been (especially with regard to theoretical and methodological justifications)
- The predicted **significance** of the research may also be only partly considered (e.g. for whom the contribution will be important or significant and why)

Feedback on the PowerPoint Slides for the Oral Presentation

Some supervisors advise their students to create PowerPoint slides before writing the confirmation proposal so that they can discuss the content and its organisation with them and thereby eliminate content that may not be relevant or that may be ineffectively organised. This approach can assist with clarifying both the relevant content and the best way in which it can be organised to create a rhetorically effective argument. If this approach is adopted, more feedback is likely to be required at this stage than if the slides are designed after the confirmation proposal document has been written.

Some of the areas in which feedback may be necessary are included in Box 2.19.

BOX 2.19 THE FOCUS OF POWERPOINT SLIDES FEEDBACK

- The content of slides may be too dense and therefore be inaccessible for a listening audience
- The design of the slides may include too many complete sentences (instead of key points or headings)
- The headings or key points may not distinguish between those that are main points and those that are subsidiary points
- The slides may focus only on descriptive content and ignore the why factor (i.e. explanations about why the descriptive material

(Continued)

---

36 Advice/Feedback in Provisional Enrolment Period

> *(Continued)*
>
> has been selected and how it contributes to the case being made in the proposal)
>
> - Tables, figures and charts need to be clear and easily navigated but sometimes it is unclear where the reader is to focus first
> - See the final chapter of this book for other aspects that may also be relevant to the oral presentation of the confirmation proposal

Having identified some of the key areas of advice and feedback that may need to be given to students during their provisional period of enrolment, we can now focus our attention in Chapter 3 on pre-writing advice that supervisors might find it is worth giving their students before they start writing the chapters of their dissertation.

3

ADVICE ON THE SELECTION OF CONTENT FOR DISSERTATION CHAPTERS

Introduction

The advice that is given to students about the type of content that is relevant to each of their chapters and the dissertation abstract depends on the purpose or functions of each chapter. If students have consciously noticed what other doctoral students have covered in their dissertations, they may have quite a good idea of the content areas expected. However, it is best to not assume anything and find out what they know in face-to-face meetings before they start to write each chapter. In these meetings, we discuss (1) their understanding of the purposes or functions of the chapter they are about to write and (2) their understanding of the types of content that will enable them to meet the purposes/functions that have been discussed. It is more often the case that students have only a partial understanding of the content areas that are typically expected. Thus, supervisors need to be prepared to articulate what they expect their students to include in each chapter. This may include a discussion of handout materials or the provision of references to various resources.

In this chapter, I focus on the advice and materials I give students before they start drafting each chapter. I begin by explaining that each chapter of a dissertation can be regarded as a part-genre of the dissertation genre and that there are certain things they should understand about what characterises the genre and its part-genres. The second part of this chapter outlines the advice I typically give on (1) the purposes/functions of each chapter and (2) the discourse move options (units of content that might be included) that students can consider so that they produce a chapter that meets the purposes/functions that have been discussed. Because of the connection between purpose/function and discourse move options, I present both of these aspects for each of the key chapters of a traditional, empirically based

38 Advice on the Selection of Content

dissertation: introduction, literature review (1 or more chapters), methodology (1 or more chapters), presentation of results, discussion of results, conclusion. The final section of this chapter refers to several strategies that can be used in the writing of each chapter of the dissertation.

Advice on the Role of Genre Knowledge

The term 'genre' has been defined in a number of ways but, in each full definition, a number of key characteristics have always been included. The first is that a genre is a type of discourse that typically occurs in a particular setting. In this case, the particular setting is an academic setting where the academic expectations and requirements of what constitutes a dissertation are defined by the academic community of researchers, teachers, examiners, supervisors and institutions. The second characteristic is the distinctive and recognisable patterns and norms with respect to the types of content that are included and to ways in which the content is organised to facilitate rhetorical clarity and effectiveness. This means that the type of content presented in one dissertation will be sufficiently similar to that found in other dissertations even when disciplinary and institutional differences and conventions have been adhered to. The third characteristic is the particular and distinctive communicative purposes and functions that determine the nature of the content and how it is organised. In this chapter, I focus only on the selection of content and leave the organisation of the content to Chapter 4.

In order to meet the specific purposes/functions of each genre, genre theory has proposed a series of discourse move options (units of content) that can be considered for inclusion in each genre. These have been identified by the research of discourse analysts and they describe what typifies the content focus of a particular part-genre. When giving students advice about these options (i.e. both the main moves and the subsidiary moves), supervisors need to explain that they are options (rather than mandatory requirements) about what has typically been observed in the research undertaken by discipline specialists. From the discipline-specific move research that has been published, more generic moves have been proposed in a number of books (e.g. Bitchener, 2010; Paltridge & Starfield, 2007), and it is these that are outlined in this chapter. These, then, are a starting point for students as they think about the type of content that they may wish to include in their dissertation chapters. Some disciplines and institutions may have conventions that mean supervisors need to advise their students against the inclusion of one or more of the optional discourse moves or advise that additional discourse moves be included in the range of options. Therefore, supervisors would do well to discuss their expectations and requirements with all students as part of the advice they give before writing commences. For additional information on how discourse moves might be included in a dissertation, Bitchener (2010) may be consulted as it includes a discourse analysis of key aspects of each chapter of a thesis that was written by a good Masters student.

Purposes/Functions and Discourse Move Options for each Dissertation Chapter

The Introduction Chapter

The generic purposes/functions and discourse move options of a typical dissertation introduction chapter are presented respectively in Box 3.1 and Table 3.1. It is important to note that the purposes or functions of an introductory chapter are discussed before the discourse move options because they inform the type of content (i.e. the discourse move options) that is appropriate for achieving these purposes and functions.

BOX 3.1 GENERIC PURPOSES/FUNCTIONS OF AN INTRODUCTION CHAPTER

1. To describe the dissertation problem, issue or question that interests you
2. To review the background and context of the problem
3. To establish what has been said and done in the problem area by referring to the theoretical, empirical and non-research literature
4. To identify gaps in the body of knowledge
5. To explain what you hope to add to this body of knowledge
6. To explain why the gaps selected for investigation are important/significant enough for investigation (the rationale and significance of the research)
7. To outline how you carried out your investigation, together with an indication of the scope and parameters of the research
8. To outline the content and structure of the dissertation

In discussing the eight purposes or functions, it is worth highlighting a few points that students should be made aware of. First, gaps in the body of knowledge should not only focus on gaps in empirical knowledge but also on theoretical and methodological gaps that may not have been considered or published in earlier literature. Second, because adding to the body of knowledge requires that an original contribution be made, consideration should therefore be given to ways in which the research may be able to contribute to theory-building (i.e. adding to existing theoretical explanations and maybe contesting or modifying existing perspectives) and to an understanding of effective methodological approaches for investigating the type of problem at the centre of the research. Third, in discussing the scope and parameters of the research, students should be acquainted with the fact that their study is a finite piece of investigation and that its parameters need to be clearly identified and justified.

40 Advice on the Selection of Content

The discourse move options in Table 3.1 may guide students in their selection of content for the chapter. The sub-moves indicate how the three main moves may be discussed. To some extent, they are sequenced to suggest how the argument might be organised but, as can be seen with the sub-moves of main move 1, little guidance is given about how the four sub-moves (a) – (d) might be inter-related and recycled. Although this will be discussed in greater detail in Chapter 4, it is worth noting here that an outline of the problem, the issue or the question that is the focus and motivation for the dissertation is best introduced at the beginning of the move.

There are a number of additional pieces of advice that I give my students when explaining the discourse move options in Table 3.1. First, terms and constructs, as they are operationalised in the dissertation, need to be clearly defined in the introduction. Sometimes students will provide a quotation from an expert in the field to indicate the defining features of the term or construct but it may not necessarily capture exactly how it has been used in the dissertation research. It may be better for students to write their own definitions and point the reader forward to the literature review chapter if a wider discussion of the terms and constructs are discussed there. The second additional piece of advice concerns the need to critically assess or evaluate every piece of descriptive literature that is presented, especially when there is some debate or

TABLE 3.1 The Discourse Move Options of an Introduction Chapter

Main moves		Sub-moves
1 Establish your research territory	a	Explain the extent to which it is important, central, interesting, problematic or relevant
	b	Provide background information about the area
	c	Introduce and review aspects of previous literature in the area (theoretical, empirical and non-research literature)
	d	Define terms and constructs on first mention
2 Establish a niche in the territory	a	Indicate a gap in the literature
	b	Raise a question about a gap in the literature
	c	Identify a problem or need
	d	Extend previous knowledge
3 Occupy the niche	a	Outline the purpose, aim, objectives of your research study
	b	Specify the research questions/hypotheses that were investigated
	c	Outline the relevant theoretical frameworks and perspectives/ positions
	d	Describe the methodology/design of your study
	e	Indicate the scope and parameters of the study
	f	Explain the likely contribution and value of the research to the field of knowledge
	g	Outline the chapter organisation of the dissertation

Advice on the Selection of Content **41**

controversy about different theoretical positions or when there are conflicting findings in the published empirical literature. The third piece of advice relates to main move three. Some disciplines may not expect that all the sub-moves be covered in the introductory chapter so it is important that supervisors give their students some advice on what is expected. For instance, some disciplines will expect a wider and deeper consideration of the sub-moves of main move 3 than other disciplines where this level of detail is kept to the methodology chapter.

The Literature Review Chapter

In discussing the purposes and functions of a dissertation literature review, presented in Box 3.2, it is important to draw students' attention to the ways in which these are similar and different to those outlined for the introductory chapter. Some clarification about the first three purposes or functions may be required. Purpose 1 refers to the empirical literature while purpose 2 refers to the theoretical literature and purpose 3 refers to any other type of literature that may be relevant to the background knowledge that the student believes the readers will need to be informed about (e.g. historical documents, reports from organisations, socio-political texts or policies, etc.). Second, informing readers about competing ideas, theories, and findings are an important part of establishing why the student's research is considered important and likely to make a contribution to the field. This is especially important with respect to resolving controversies and discrepancies. The final point to emphasise when discussing the purposes and functions of the literature review is the need for purpose 7 to be explicit about the connection between research questions/ hypotheses and the literature that has been presented. There can be a tendency for some students to not make this connection so supervisors would do well to be up front about this and explain that each research question/ hypothesis needs to be seen to have arisen from what has been said in the literature sections.

BOX 3.2 GENERIC PURPOSES/FUNCTIONS OF A LITERATURE REVIEW CHAPTER

1   To review the research literature relevant to the study
2   To review the theoretical perspectives that underpin or inform the research
3   To review any non-research literature (e.g. reports, etc.) that summarises and synthesises background and contextual information

(Continued)

42 Advice on the Selection of Content

> *(Continued)*
>
> 4 To critique 1–3 above by (a) identifying arguments for and against issues and controversies and (b) weighing up the value of various theories, arguments, claims, conclusions, methodologies/designs (including an identification of strengths and weaknesses)
> 5 To identify gaps or shortcomings in this knowledge
> 6 To justify why the gap(s) are important and significant enough to be investigated
> 7 To explain how the design and execution of your research was informed by the above activities (e.g. how the literature provided a focus for your research questions/hypotheses and guided your methodology and design)

In discussing the discourse move options of the literature review (identified in Table 3.2), supervisors should draw their students' attention to similarities with the discourse move options of the introductory chapter.

The move options provide a macro view of what the content of the literature will include but they do not tell the student much about the specific areas

TABLE 3.2 The Discourse Move Options of a Literature Review Chapter

Main moves		Sub-moves
1 Establish some aspect of the knowledge territory relevant to your research	a	Present knowledge claims and statements about theories, beliefs, constructs and definitions
	b	Explain the centrality, importance or significance of the area of knowledge
	c	Present the research evidence (e.g. findings, methodology)
2 Create a research niche/gap in knowledge	a	Critique knowledge claims, issues, problems associated with move 1 claims/statements; present research evidence to support each critique
	b	Identify gaps in knowledge/research
	c	Explain any continuation or development of traditions that have been established but not fully investigated
	d	Present arguments for introducing any new perspective or theoretical framework (as a result of move 1 claims)
3 Announce how you will occupy the research niche/gap	a	Announce the aim(s) of your study
	b	Announce the relevant theoretical position(s) or framework(s)
	c	Announce the key research design and processes
	d	Announce how you defined key concepts and terms in your study

of content that might be included. Thus, the writing of the literature review can be a student's 'bête noire'. The extent to which supervisors should guide their students about the content of the review is not an easy one to advise on. Some supervisors prefer to let their students discover for themselves what should be included while others prefer to offer specific guidelines about what they expect. My preference tends to fall between these two approaches. I prefer students to come up with a detailed table of contents about what they plan to include and then have a discussion with them about what has been suggested, about the organisation of the various suggestions, and about any additional sections or sub-sections the student should consider including. Perhaps the most important discussion to have is about how the areas of selected content are going to be organised to create an argument that leads to a position that informed the need for some aspect of the research. In Chapter 4, more attention will be given to the creation of argument. Some supervisors may want to include some of the ideas of Chapter 4 in their pre-writing advice but others may prefer to refer to this material only if a student's text warrants it.

Because knowledge critique is so important and is typically so poorly done, advice should be given to students before they write their literature review about (1) what it means to critique the ideas and findings of others and (2) about why it is important.

The relative importance of the three main discourse moves of literature reviews in the discipline should also be discussed because often the third move may only occupy one or two paragraphs at the end of the literature review rather than a more lengthy statement. Supervisors should clarify what the expectations of their discipline are.

Before students start writing their literature review, I find it is useful to deconstruct one major section of a dissertation literature review and discuss the cyclical nature of the sub-moves for the first two main moves, given that each of these main moves will comprise a number of relevant and related sections, with each focusing on a major area of literature that is relevant to backgrounding one of the research questions/hypotheses. Deconstructing and discussing how one student writer has repeatedly drawn upon or recycled the various sub-moves and seeing how they inter-relate can be a very useful approach when giving advice on the writing of this chapter.

In Box 3.3, an example of some of the key sub-move options that the student recycled has been provided to illustrate their interplay. In this excerpt from a dissertation on the willingness of learners to communicate in the second language learning classroom, the student is continuing a discussion of the early literature on the role of motivation in determining whether or not learners are willing to initiate communication.

44 Advice on the Selection of Content

BOX 3.3 AN EXAMPLE OF THE INTERPLAY OF SUB-MOVE OPTIONS

A noticeable 'educational shift' occurred in motivation research during the 1990s, a period of feverish research	Move a (critique)
activity in L2 learning motivation. In particular, the period was marked by a search for new learning motivation paradigms, as well as an expansion of the scope, in both theory and practice, of L2 learning motivation.	Moves 2a, 2e (critique & new perspective)
The most influential pioneering works were provided by Crookes and Schmidt (1991), Dornyei (1994), Oxford and Shearin (1994). Crookes and Schmidt (1991) criticised the dominance of Gardner's social psychological	Move 2a (critique)
approach, offering instead a motivational framework made up of four components. These were interest, relevance, expectancy and satisfaction/outcome. According	Moves 21, 2e (critique & new perspective)
to the authors, these variables provided an alternative to Gardner's integrative/instrumental dichotomy (Dornyei, 2001). Dornyei (1994) criticised Gardner's model because, in his view, its main emphasis relied on general motivational components grounded in a social milieu rather than in the foreign language classroom. He therefore called for a more pragmatic and education-centred approach to language learning motivation. In this he followed an approach taken earlier by Crookes and Schmidt (1991), by examining motivation at micro, classroom curriculum and extracurricular levels, then synthesising them into a three-level framework – language level, learner level and learning situation level. Oxford and Shearin's (1994) study addressed a	Move 2a (critique) Moves 2a, 2e (critique & new perspective)
growing gap between L2 motivation theories and the emerging concepts in mainstream motivational psychology. They argued that the integrative/instrumental	Moves 2a, 2b (critique & evidence)
view of motivation was too narrow, and offered alternative ways by which the notion of L2 motivation might be considered. Yet, at the same time, they called for an expansion of the social psychological approach. A common thread running through the literature mentioned above was a view suggesting that Gardner's theory was so influential and dominant, that alternative concepts were not seriously considered (Crookes & Schmidt, 1991; Dornyei, 1994).	Moves 2a, 2e (critique & new perspective)

Advice on the Selection of Content **45**

The Methodology Chapter

Students are likely to be familiar with the content focus of methodology chapters either from their reading of other dissertations or from their reading of journal articles that report empirical research. The following purposes or functions in Box 3.4 are unlikely to be misunderstood, especially when they are considered together with the discourse moves presented in Table 3.3. Nevertheless, the importance of the word 'justify' should be emphasised as many first iterations of this chapter can be thin on why certain processes and procedures have been adopted and why they are appropriate.

BOX 3.4 GENERIC PURPOSES/FUNCTIONS OF A METHODOLOGY CHAPTER

1   To describe and justify the methodological approach best suited to your research questions/hypotheses
2   To describe and justify the research design best suited to examine your research questions/hypotheses
3   To describe and justify the specific methods employed for data collection
4   To explain how the validity and reliability or truthfulness of your data were achieved
5   To describe and justify your data collection procedures
6   To describe and justify your data analysis procedures

It is useful to have a discussion about some of the discourse moves included in Table 3.3 because students and supervisors may have different understandings of what is intended. First, the methodological approach component of the chapter should include a philosophical discussion of the approach that is relevant to the focus of the research (e.g. post-positivist; epistemological, etc.) and why it is the appropriate approach for the types of research questions/hypotheses that were investigated. This may lead to a discussion about why a mixed methods approach, a qualitative approach or a quantitative approach was employed and then to an outline of the specific methods that were used to obtain data for answering the research questions or for testing any hypotheses.

The second piece of advice that is worth giving students before they start writing this chapter concerns the level of detail that the descriptive parts of the chapter should include. Because this is a dissertation and not a journal article, students are expected to demonstrate the breadth and depth of their knowledge. Thus, for example, if they are describing and justifying the referential statistics they used to determine the significance of their findings, they will be expected

46 Advice on the Selection of Content

TABLE 3.3 The Discourse Move Options of a Methodology Chapter

Main moves	Sub-moves
1 Present the procedures for measuring the variables of your research	a Describe and justify the methodological approach of the study from a philosophical perspective b Define, describe and justify the methods of measuring the variables of your study
2 Explain the data collection procedures	a Describe the sample (e.g. location, size, characteristics, context, ethical issues) b Describe the instruments used for data collection; describe the validity and reliability or truthfulness measures c Describe the steps of the data collection procedures d Justify a–c, highlighting advantages and disadvantages, in light of research aim(s) and research questions/hypotheses
3 Explain the data analysis procedures	a Describe/illustrate and justify the data analysis procedures

to not only describe the tests that were used but also to justify why they were the appropriate ones for the data of the study.

Readers of a methodology chapter should feel confident that they would be able to replicate the study if they chose to. This means, therefore, that all steps need to be identified. It is important to mention this to students because they will often leave out a critical piece of information that is needed so that step 2 can follow on from step 1, for example.

The Presentation of Results Chapter

There is nothing difficult to understand about the purpose or functions of a chapter such as presented in Box 3.5 that simply presents the findings or results of the research.

BOX 3.5 GENERIC PURPOSES/FUNCTIONS OF A RESULTS CHAPTER

1 To present the results/findings of your study that are relevant to your research questions/hypotheses
2 To explain what the findings mean (without interpretation and discussion)
3 To present evidence in support of your findings

Advice on the Selection of Content **47**

TABLE 3.4 The Discourse Move Options of a Results Chapter

Main moves	*Sub-moves*	
1 Present briefly any meta-textual information	a	Present any background information, methodological detail, references forward to the discussion chapter and links between sections that contextualise the results to be presented
2 Present the results	a	Restate the research question/hypothesis
	b	Present briefly any important procedures for generating the results that the reader should be reminded of
	c	Present each result
	d	Provide evidence for each result (e.g. statistics, examples, tables, figures)
	e	Explain what each result means

A chapter that simply presents results or findings is not difficult to write if a decision has been made about how the various findings are to be sequenced. A discussion about whether they will be presented chronologically according to the order of the research question/hypothesis or more thematically would be worth having before students start to write the chapter. Students should be advised to avoid **discussing** the findings if the chapter is solely about **presenting** what the findings were.

Main move 1, in Table 3.4, suggests that meta-textual information might be provided at the beginning of the chapter. Some disciplines and supervisors will advise that this be given so that readers who are not reading the chapter immediately after having read the preceding chapters are reminded of background information that they should be mindful of when reading the chapter. Other disciplines and supervisors may advise against incorporating this background information if they are happy for readers to refer back to it in an earlier chapter. Thus, it is worth discussing with students what your expectations are in this regard.

The Discussion of Results Chapter

The first purpose stated in Box 3.6 contextualises the two main purposes (2 and 3). Some disciplines may not consider this to be an important part of the chapter so it would be wise for supervisors to clarify their expectations with students before they start to write the chapter. Having presented the findings of the investigation in the previous chapter, the discussion chapter can then focus on why the findings occurred as they did and on how they might compare with those of other related studies introduced in the literature review chapter. Students should be clear that such a discussion will not only refer to earlier empirical studies but also consider theoretical and methodological explanations.

48 Advice on the Selection of Content

BOX 3.6 GENERIC PURPOSES/FUNCTIONS OF A DISCUSSION OF RESULTS CHAPTER

1 To provide a brief overview of the aim(s) of the research, of the theoretical and research contexts of the research and of the methodological approach for investigating the research questions/hypotheses
2 To interpret your results, compare them with other research results, and explain why they occurred as they did
3 To discuss the contribution you believe your results have made to the research questions/hypotheses, to theory-building, to new empirical knowledge and to practice

---

The range of discourse move options outlined in Table 3.5 provides specific guidance for the student on what is typically included in a discussion of findings chapter. Again, the first move provides a contextual introduction that may or may not be considered necessary. For each of the findings, the wide range of discourse 3 sub-moves can be drawn upon for the discussion. Depending on the importance and significance of a finding, in relation to the focus of the research question, some of the sub-move options may not be relevant. For example, sub-move (g) on making suggestions for further research and sub-move (h) on justifying why further research is recommended may be more relevant

TABLE 3.5 The Discourse Move Options of a Discussion of Results Chapter

Main moves	Sub-moves
1 Provide any background information considered important for understanding the discussion	a Restate aim(s), research questions/hypotheses, key research and methodological approach
2 Present a statement of result	a Restate a key result b Expand statement about the key result
3 Evaluate/comment on each result	a Explain the result by suggesting reasons for it b Explain whether the result was expected or unexpected c Compare the result with the results of previous research d Provide examples of the result e Make a more general claim arising from the result, draw a conclusion or state a hypothesis f Quote previous research to support (e) g Make suggestions for further research h Justify why further research is recommended

Advice on the Selection of Content **49**

to a discussion of several findings than to a discussion of an individual finding, and sub-move (e) on making a more general claim arising from a result, drawing a conclusion or stating a hypothesis may not always include a conclusion even though it may make a claim. The advice I give my students is to consider each of the sub-move options and reach a decision about why each one should or should not be included in the discussion. Finally, students' attention should be drawn to the fact that there is a logic to the way in which these sub-moves have been sequenced. The sequencing of sub-moves will be considered further in Chapter 5 where the focus is on argumentation.

The Conclusion Chapter

It is often the case that the conclusion chapter is read in isolation from other chapters by both students and academics. Sometimes, this may occur because readers want an overview of the dissertation in order to decide whether or not they will read the whole work. Thus, if the purposes identified in Box 3.7 inform the writing of the conclusion chapter, readers seeking a summary outline will receive the type of overview of the dissertation that a reading of the introduction chapter alone would not be able to provide. Depending on the level of attention given to the contribution of the findings to the field in the discussion chapter, purpose 3 (contribution to the field) may be a highly developed discussion or it may be more of an overview of what has been provided in the discussion chapter. This part of the dissertation is arguably the most important part because it tells the reader what the research has to offer the field of knowledge. Given its importance, it is surprising that so many students fail to give it the status and detailed attention it needs. Other purposes of the conclusion chapter, as listed in Box 3.7, are easier for students to write about, so little pre-writing advice may be required on these.

BOX 3.7   GENERIC PURPOSES/FUNCTIONS OF A CONCLUSION CHAPTER

1   To remind the reader of the aim(s), research questions/hypotheses and methodological features of your study
2   To summarise your key findings
3   To evaluate the importance and significance of your study with a commentary on its contribution to the field (i.e. to theory-building, to new empirical knowledge, to methodological advancements, and to practice
4   To identify limitations of the study (both in terms of weaknesses/flaws and scope/parameters)
5   To identify areas for further research
6   To identify practical applications

50 Advice on the Selection of Content

TABLE 3.6 The Discourse Move Options of a Conclusion Chapter

Main moves	Sub-moves
1 Restate aims and methodological approach of the study	a Restate the aim(s), research questions/hypotheses b Restate key features of the research methodology and methods
2 Summarise key results	a Provide a summary of the key findings of the study
3 Evaluate the study's contribution to the field (theory, new knowledge, methodology and practice)	a Comment on the significance of the study for theory-building, developing new empirical knowledge, developing new methodological approaches and for practical application b Justify each comment for (a)
4 Identify limitations and areas for further research	a Identify any limitations (weaknesses/flaws and scope/parameters) b Recommend and justify areas for further research

The discourse move options in Table 3.6 follow the sequence given in the purposes of the chapter outlined in Box 3.7. Thus, little advice should be needed about what the main and sub-move options mean, apart from a reminder perhaps of the importance of justifying everything that is included in the chapter.

The Abstract

The purposes and discourse move options of the abstract have been placed at the end of this chapter because the abstract lies outside the dissertation itself and because it is typically written towards the end of the writing journey. The five purposes identified in Box 3.8 are intended to give a clear overview of the focus of the dissertation. Some disciplines highlight the importance of some of these purposes more than others so it is important for supervisors to clarify what is expected. In some disciplines, for example, purposes 2 and 5 may be omitted altogether. Purposes 3 and 4 are typically considered of much importance across disciplines and may occupy four-fifths of the space allocated to the abstract. Apart from signalling what students are expected to cover, the best advice might arise from a discussion of a deconstructed model of an effective abstract.

BOX 3.8 GENERIC PURPOSES/FUNCTIONS OF AN ABSTRACT

1 To outline the aims of the study
2 To describe the background and context of the study
3 To describe the methodology and methods used in the study
4 To present the key findings of the study
5 To comment on the contribution of the study to the field of knowledge

Advice on the Selection of Content **51**

TABLE 3.7 The Discourse Move Options of an Abstract

Main moves	Sub -moves	
1 Introduction	a	Outline background, context of the study
	b	Explain the motivation for the research
	c	Explain the significance and centrality of the research focus
	d	Identify the knowledge gap(s) or need for the continuation of a tradition
2 Purpose	a	Identify the aims or intentions, research questions/hypotheses
	b	Develop aspects of (a)
3 Method	a	Identify and justify the methodological approach and methods
	b	Identify key design aspects
	c	Identify data sources
	d	Identify data analysis processes
4 Product	a	Present main findings of research questions/hypotheses
5 Conclusion	a	Suggest significance/importance of the findings to the field
	b	Identify any important limitations
	c	Make recommendations for further research

If the range of discourse sub-move options outlined in Table 3.7 were to be included in an abstract, it is likely that the text would cover two or three pages. Thus, advice may need to be given to students about which of these are considered to be more important in the discipline. Some of the sub-move options can, of course, be combined within a single statement (e.g. sub-moves of main moves 1 and 3). The writing of an abstract requires a level of skill that some students may struggle with, so, even though the abstract text is much smaller than that of the other texts they will have written, supervisors and students should not be concerned if several iterations are required.

Strategies for the Writing of each Chapter

The focus of this chapter has been on the purposes/functions of each chapter and on the type of content that each of the chapters may include. Guidelines on the type of content or the areas of content that might be expected in each chapter have also been provided in the form of discourse move options. For some students, this advice may be a little too abstract or theoretical so the remainder of this chapter offers some advice on how supervisors might 'add flesh to the bones' of what has been provided so far.

Deconstructing Model Examples

Model examples of sections of a chapter, or indeed of a whole chapter, can either be given to students or they can be asked to select one or more from their reading programme. What they are asked to do with the sample may vary from student to student, from supervisor to supervisor and from chapter to chapter.

52 Advice on the Selection of Content

Because I am supervising a large number of doctoral students, my approach is to bring the cohort together for a session in which sections or chapter samples are deconstructed and discussed. This means that students need to have been given the text before the meeting so that they have had time to read it and they also need to have reflected upon what they consider to be noteworthy features of the content. The same approach could be followed with just one student but the richness of what emerges from a group discussion would be less likely to surface. It is important that the discussion of the sample text includes reference to the discourse moves. An example of this can be found in Bitchener (2010) where parts of chapters are discussed in terms of the extent to which they illustrate the use of a particular discourse move and its various sub-moves. For some students, it may be helpful if the supervisor provides a small piece of text (e.g. a sub-section of a major section within a chapter) and discusses a discourse move analysis that has been undertaken of that piece of text before giving students the opportunity to do the same with another small piece of text. This can be done in pairs or in small groups before a plenary discussion. This approach should ensure that students clearly understand what is involved in the approach. An example of this approach was provided earlier in Box 3.3.

Create a Table of Contents

As I have mentioned elsewhere in this book, the creation and discussion of a table of contents is one way to ensure that students are going to focus on content that is relevant to the purposes/functions of the chapter that they are planning to write. The more detailed the table is, that is, the more headings and sub-headings there are, the more certain a supervisor can be that the student is likely to be focused throughout the writing process. If there is any doubt about this, it may be useful if the student writes up one part of the table of contents first and then seeks the supervisor's feedback before writing the other parts outlined in the table of contents. An example of a table of contents was referred to earlier in Chapter 2 of this book.

Write an Argument Overview

Another approach that will reveal the extent to which the selected content is relevant to the focus of a chapter is one which asks students to write an extended paragraph overview of a chapter or of a section of the chapter. Sometimes, this is described as an advance organiser. Not only does this type of argument overview signal the range of content that will be included in the chapter or section, but it also reveals the relationship between areas of content. More will be said about the argument structure in Chapter 5 of this book. An example of an argument overview was referred to earlier in Chapter 2 of this book.

Write Iterations of Sections of the Whole Chapter

Once feedback has been provided on the content included in the first iteration of a section of a chapter, further advice can then be provided on any areas of content that need to be added, modified or deleted. Once a section of a chapter has developed from a table of contents to a completed text, it can then be seen whether or not such modifications may be required but, having initially provided a detailed table of contents, it is unlikely that many modifications and revised iterations will be required.

4

FEEDBACK ON THE SELECTION OF CONTENT FOR DISSERTATION CHAPTERS

Introduction

This chapter focuses on the feedback that supervisors often find they need to give their dissertation students about the selection of content that they have included in their chapters. If students have been given the type of advice outlined in Chapter 3, the amount of post-writing feedback required should be less than that which would be required if it had not been given. However, the effective application of advice may be something that takes some learners longer to achieve than others. It should be noted that the use that students make of the content they select for their chapters will be the focus of Chapter 5 where consideration is given to both pre-writing advice and post-writing feedback that students may need to be given on the coherence of the arguments they present from the content that has been selected.

The amount of feedback that supervisors may need to provide on a chapter will often depend on when the chapter has been written. Early drafts are likely to require more feedback and it is for this reason that it is probably best to focus only on the selection of content first rather than focusing concurrently on other areas of concern. However, if students only require a limited amount of feedback, it may not be too early to start focusing on how they use the content to present their arguments. As each new iteration is completed, less and less feedback should be required on the selection of content.

The feedback that is often given by supervisors on the early drafts of the six chapters of a traditional, empirically based dissertation is discussed in this chapter.

The Introduction Chapter

Students will often write an initial draft of their introduction chapter after they have completed the literature review for their confirmation proposal and revise it in at least two further iterations. The first of these iterations will be written after the literature review chapter of the dissertation has been written and before the research data have been collected and analysed. The reason for this is to ensure that students minimise the chance that a more detailed literature after the data have been collected does not lead to any regrets about having not included in the design additional factors that the literature has drawn their attention to. The second of these iterations will be written after the results chapter has been written and before the findings are discussed. This is to ensure that any additional literature that might be needed to explain the results is added to the review so that it can then be referred to in the discussion of the findings. The literature component of the introduction chapter may then be revised once a comprehensive revision of the literature review chapter has been commented on. As well, a final revision of the introduction chapter is best considered once the conclusion chapter has been written. This is to ensure that each of these chapters aligns with the focus of the other.

So what are the content selection issues that supervisors often find it necessary to provide feedback on?

The Nature and Scope of the Problem that the Research Investigates

Defining and explaining clearly the problem that the research investigates can be a challenge for some students. This may be because they are unclear themselves and need to do more reading. Often, the first iteration of the problem statement will be too broad and/or too vague. However, this issue can be resolved once it has been pointed out as an issue by the supervisor, or when more reading has been completed. I often find that asking questions of students in an oral feedback meeting helps them to focus more specifically on what the central issue of the problem is. Asking questions about what is meant by the terms and/or constructs that they have referred to can also help this process, as indeed can a discussion of how the scope of the problem could be narrowed to something that is more manageable for a doctoral dissertation, as opposed to one's life's work. As one supervisor once said to me, students sometimes also need to be told that 'it is unnecessary for them to go back to Aristotle'. I find once we start discussing the research questions that they plan to investigate, this helps students to sharpen their understanding of the focus of the problem that informs the various research questions. This discussion can also lead to an elimination of some of the questions and/or some of the components of individual questions.

The Rationale and Importance or Significance of the Problem

Being able to articulate the rationale or reason(s) for focusing on a particular problem is important if students are to investigate not only a gap in knowledge

56 Feedback on the Selection of Content

but also identify one that is of importance for advancing new knowledge in the field. Sometimes they need to be told that not every gap or issue is worth investigating. In the first instance, if students have not thought carefully about the rationale and the importance or significance of the problem they have identified and have not explained this clearly and completely enough in their introduction, I draw their attention to this in my written feedback and follow up on it with a face-to-face discussion after they have read and thought about my comments. Most often, at this stage of their thinking, students are able to make one or two valid points about ways in which they think their research may be significant for the field. A face-to-face discussion of these points can lead to a realisation that there are other ways in which their findings may also be significant. Thus, the aim of the follow-up meetings such as this is to extend this thinking.

The Context of the Problem

Students tend to understand that it is important to situate the problem or issue they are focusing on in their research within the wider context of knowledge but sometimes their literature background is not extensive enough to be able to do this so they may need to be guided about how to extend their knowledge base. As a result, they are likely to struggle with a sufficiently comprehensive statement on both the rationale and importance or significance of the problem. Additionally, while students usually seem to understand that a gap in knowledge can be identified in the empirical research literature, they often focus only on this as a reason for their problem focus. Some students will make glib reference to theoretical reasons for focusing on a particular problem but many need to have their attention drawn to the importance of considering the theoretical rationale for focusing on the problem they have selected. If the theoretical framework has been clearly conceived when the first full version of the literature review has been written, it is less likely that students will ignore this component of the rationale in their introduction chapter. More will be said about the theoretical conceptualisation issues in the next section on the literature review chapter.

The Content Balance

Following the point just made about the limited attention that may be given to the theoretical framework of a student's research, it is not surprising that there is sometimes an imbalance between empirical and theoretical reasons for focusing on a particular problem. Typically, attention will need to be drawn to an over-abundance of literature on empirical findings and a somewhat sketchy consideration of the theoretical basis for focusing on the problem. This is not altogether surprising because the empirical literature is often more accessible compared with the amount of time it can take to access and reflect on theoretical literature that is relevant to the research focus of the proposal.

How the Problem Is Investigated

Once the problem has been identified, described and justified as one that is worthy of investigation, the introduction chapter should signal the key aims or the research questions/hypotheses of the student's study. Conventions across disciplines can vary so the manner in which this is done needs to be understood by the student and pointed out by the supervisor if necessary. Some expect that the specific focus of the investigation will be signalled with statements of aim while others expect that the research questions or hypotheses to be tested will be stated as such. The amount of attention given to an overview of how the problem is to be carried out also tends to vary from discipline to discipline, with some requiring a relatively detailed introduction to the key components of the methodology chapter and others requiring only a sentence or two that directs readers to what is presented at the end of the literature review chapter(s) or in the methodology chapter itself.

The Originality and Significance of the Contribution to the Field

Arguably, this is the most important part of the introduction chapter but, unfortunately, it tends to be the most frequently ignored or the most poorly considered. While it is understood that students will increase their understanding of the significance of their work as they proceed, it should still be possible for them to articulate some aspirational goals in terms of what they believe their original contribution might be – at least in terms of new empirical knowledge and methodological contributions, even if an understanding of their contribution to theory-building is tentative. At minimum, an early draft of the introduction chapter should be able to identify what the student hopes to add to the body of knowledge. Written feedback in the form of key questions, designed to elicit this information, is one useful way of focusing students' attention on this lacuna and of asking them to think about it before a face-to-face feedback meeting.

The Personal Voice

The extent to which students engage with the problem and reflect upon what it means to them will largely determine the extent to which a personal voice is evident in the chapter. Some disciplines expect this characteristic to be evident in the introduction while others consider it to be optional. Supervisors who wish to encourage this involvement can suggest that their students think about whether there are any personal circumstances that led them to an interest in the field of study. A number of my doctoral students are interested in investigating the potential of written corrective feedback for second language development because, as second language writers and often as teachers of second language

58 Feedback on the Selection of Content

writers in a mother tongue context, they have been exposed to various feedback practices that may or may not have been particularly effective. Thus, they have a strong personal motivation for wanting to play a part in the on-going research into the potential of such for feedback for learning a second language. Given their interest in this area of research, a personal statement about why they are interested in studying written corrective feedback should be seen as an important part of the wider rationale statement they present in the introduction chapter. It is therefore appropriate that their personal voice be identified.

The Literature Review Chapter

The literature review may be presented in one or more chapters. In the Social Sciences and Humanities, it often occupies two chapters, with one being devoted to the theoretical conceptualisation of the research and the other to the empirical and non-research components of the research. In this section of this feedback chapter, my discussion of feedback typically given to students will consider the literature review as one chapter rather than as two or more chapters.

Before writing the literature review chapter of the dissertation, students will have written a literature review for their confirmation proposal (see Chapter 2). Depending on how thorough their reading has been and how effective their review of the reading has been, these two factors will determine the nature and amount of feedback they are given on the first full iteration of the review for the dissertation.

The literature review is typically regarded as the most difficult chapter for students to write, not only because it serves a variety of purposes and spans a large amount of text but also because it draws upon a wide range of reading, thinking and writing skills, not to mention a critical stance with regard to the literature that is presented. While the organisation and structure of the argument of the review is typically more problematic for many students than the selection of content, our attention in this chapter is on the latter. The issues that supervisors frequently find it necessary to give feedback on, especially on the first full draft, are discussed now in this section. As we saw in the previous section on the introduction chapter, macro issues are best dealt with first.

The Selection of Content

First and foremost, the content needs to be relevant to the focus of the problem or the research questions. As such, the content may include non-research literature (e.g. reports, documents related to the wider context of the subject of the research) as well as research literature (both theoretical and empirical). Coverage of the non-research literature and the empirical literature tends to be less problematic for students but their consideration of the theoretical perspectives relevant to the focus of the research (indicated by the focus of the research questions) is often more of a challenge for some students. Feedback on the latter may often include not only guidance on what theoretical literature to consider from within the field in which the student is working but also direction about relevant theoretical literature from other disciplines. In my own field of expertise (the contribution of written corrective feedback for second language development), students often fail to consider the theoretical literature outside the wider field of second language teaching and learning when seeking answers to questions about the impact of individual, psychological factors on the cognitive processing of linguistic information. As students reflect upon whether certain pieces of literature are directly relevant to the focus of their research, I find it helps my students if they have a hardcopy of their research questions attached to their computers as a reminder to ask themselves whether each piece of literature should be included. It is generally assumed that supervisors of a particular dissertation have, to some extent at least, a relatively wide knowledge of the literature relevant to their student's research and that they can identify gaps in their student's selection of content and direct them to literature they believe they should consider including.

The Amount of Literature

Literature reviews can easily take on a life of their own and become too expansive. More often than not, the amount of detail given on the empirical literature will be a key reason for this. Some students think that they need to present information on every component of a published study rather than selecting only that which directly relates to the key idea they are writing about. More will be said about this in the next chapter on argumentation. Another issue concerning the amount of literature selected is how up-to-date it needs to be. It sometimes needs to be pointed out to students that some of their older literature can be summarised or just referenced with other literature if more recent publications have drawn on or referred to the older literature. As a ballpark guide to the size of the literature review, I suggest that it should not exceed a third the length of the dissertation. In order to work this out in terms of word count, supervisors and students need to be familiar with the optimal word count of a doctoral dissertation at their university.

Critical Engagement with the Literature

There can sometimes be a tendency for students to accept everything they read as 'gospel truth'. The willingness to accept research findings, claims and conclusions as valid, reliable and generalisable is all too common in early iterations of a literature review. Some students, even at doctoral level, are inexperienced in critically evaluating and assessing what they read. This applies not only to the empirical literature but even more so to the theoretical literature. With regard to

60 Feedback on the Selection of Content

assessing the robustness of empirical findings that are reported in the literature, my feedback frequently focuses on (1) asking students to what extent the conclusions that an author makes are based on the findings that have been reported and (2) on whether the findings are informed by a sound and robust research methodology. With regard to the theoretical literature, students may fail to critically assess the premises informing the claims of a theoretical position and fail to weigh up the value and credibility of alternative or contradictory theoretical positions before informing the reader about the stance or position they have taken in their research. Written feedback may need to question the basis upon which the perspective that students have adopted or have framed their research within has been reached. As support for both theoretically based and empirically based claims, informing the perspective they have chosen, students often make quite extensive use of citations but they are not always used effectively for the purpose of arguing or justifying their choice. Many universities provide seminars and workshops on critically assessing or evaluating literature so supervisors would do well to recommend such sessions to their students.

The Methodology Chapter

Students begin thinking about the methodology they will use to investigate their research questions while reading the literature for their initial and confirmation proposals. While feedback may have been given on these documents, it is not until they are required to write up a first full version of their methodology chapter that other issues (as well as a recurrence of those earlier commented on in Chapter 2) may emerge. The first iteration of the methodology chapter needs to be completed before students embark upon their research if they are to be sure that additional options, as a result of further reading, will not emerge once the research has commenced or more critically when it has been completed. I often find that my students want to start their data collection as soon as they have been confirmed in the doctoral programme but when I explain to them the need to complete a detailed full version of their methodology chapter, to prevent 'I wish I had considered X' comments, they usually understand the rationale behind this requirement. Once students have submitted the first full version of their methodology chapter, supervisors often find that there are a number of issues on which they need to provide feedback.

Areas Not Covered in the Chapter

Even though students are advised before writing the methodology chapter to show me a list of the key headings (i.e. the key areas of content) they will include in their chapter, they sometimes fail to identify all of the necessary areas. For example, trustworthiness (validity and reliability) is one area that is frequently

Feedback on the Selection of Content **61**

not included. Another area is a philosophical explanation and justification of the methodological approach considered relevant to the focus of their study. While students typically have no difficulty commenting and justifying the qualitative, quantitative or mixed methods approaches of their planned research, they often don't realise the need to justify these approaches with a discussion of the philosophical approach that is relevant to the aims of the research and therefore to reasons why a qualitative, quantitative or missed methods approach is appropriate. In my feedback, I typically draw their attention to good examples from other dissertations and suggest that they also consult research methodology texts. From years of examining doctoral dissertations, it has become clear that supervisors have not always focused on the importance of these explanations and justifications. For this reason, I present in Box 4.1 an example of one such statement that could be discussed with students. In this example, the student explains the appropriateness of the post-positivist approach for research that seeks to find out whether certain factors might have a moderating effect (cause and effect) on outcomes like modified accuracy in second language writing.

BOX 4.1 AN EXAMPLE OF A PHILOSOPHICAL APPROACH STATEMENT

Post positivism is the philosophy underpinning this exploration of the efficacy of written CF on acquisition and the potential moderation of feedback types, L2 motivation, and types of revision, as well as the possible causes for any significant differences in benefit from written CF. It assumes the existence of an objective social reality external to human minds, and 'this reality is only imperfectly knowable both because of the inevitable imperfection of human knowledge and because of the very nature of its laws, which are probabilistic' (Corbetta, 2001, p. 20). Hence, on the one hand, the ontology of post positivism is realism as it assumes the cause–effect relationships existing in reality outside of human minds. On the other hand, it is critical as it holds that every scientific acquisition is open to question.

As a result, the corresponding epistemology is 'modified dualism-objectivity' in pursuing 'the middle range, probabilistic and conjectural laws' (Corbetta, 2001, p. 20). Such an epistemology recognises the possible disturbing effects of the researcher on the object of study, which may lead to a reactive effect, thus holding that the goal of research for the objectivity of knowledge can only be achieved approximately. It also considers the laws generated from the research are 'limited in scope, probabilistic and provisional' (Corbetta, 2001, p. 20).

(Continued)

62 Feedback on the Selection of Content

(Continued)

Aligned with such an ontology and epistemology, the methodology is modified experimental-manipulative. In operation, measures are taken for 'a substantial detachment between the researcher and the object studied', but qualitative methods can be included (Corbetta, 2001, p. 20).

Underpinned by such a philosophy, a quasi-experiment and a multi-case study will be conducted to address the research questions. The following sections will detail their methodological approaches, participants and contexts, data collection instruments, data collection procedures, measures to enhance validity and reliability/trustworthiness of each study, and methods of data analysis. As the quasi-experiment will precede the multi-case study, details of the former will be presented first.

As 'quantification represents a reality for a group' (Selinger & Shohamy, 1989, p. 115), quantitative research is appropriate to explore the efficacy of written CF on acquisition and the moderation of feedback types, revision types, and L2 motivation. 'In particular, experiments are designed to provide clearly observable links between experimentally manipulated causes and well-defined outcomes that serve as effects' (Morgan, 2014, p. 56). Hence, an experiment design suits the thesis' purpose to explore the efficacy of written CF on acquisition and the impact of possible moderating factors.

However, it is impossible to prevent participants from being exposed to L2 input outside the experiment during its period. As quasi-experiments also seek to control the non-experimental influences for a greater confidence in the application of the treatment to other L2 learners of the same basic characteristics (Morgan, 2014), it is considered both feasible and suitable for the purpose of this study. This is true particularly in the sense that to explore the moderation of revision types and L2 motivation with written CF, these two variables will not be manipulated as they are under the control of the learners, but only be measured in this study.

Hence, a quasi-experiment will be conducted to address research questions 1–4, for these research questions involve the manipulation of independent variables and measurement of independent variables in determining any significant effects on the dependent variables.

Insufficient Descriptive Detail for a Replication of the Research

There are frequently gaps in the information provided in this chapter on processes and procedures. While students often know in great detail what they did when conducting their research, they often fail to report all of the steps and procedures. I often find myself asking them, for example, how they moved from the activity referred to in sentence one to the activity referred to in sentence two and how they defined or operationalised a key construct. I explain in my feedback that readers of the chapter need to be able to replicate their study if they want to, using the detail that they have presented and that, if they are unable to progress from one stage to another, it is likely to be because they have not been given sufficiently detailed information. An example of this problem can be seen in Box 4.2 below where a small excerpt from the data analysis section of a methodology chapter is presented. It can be seen that readers who want to replicate this type of analysis may have difficulty doing so given the lack of detail with regard to (1) what obligatory occasion analysis is and how it is applied to the student's data, (2) what the revised version of the index of accuracy included and (3) what constitutes 'overuse'.

BOX 4.2   AN EXAMPLE OF INSUFFICIENT METHODOLOGICAL DETAIL

An index of accuracy (obligatory occasion analysis with consideration of overuse) was calculated based on similar calculations used in previous research. In two studies (Shintani & Ellis, 2013; Shintani, Ellis & Suzuki, 2014) where there was a possibility to overuse the target feature, a revised version of this index of accuracy was adopted with consideration being given to overuse. As there are possibilities to overuse both of the target features in this study, the same revised version of obligatory occasion analysis was adopted.

Insufficient Justification of the Descriptive Detail

As well as providing a detailed explanation of processes and procedures, the methodology chapter needs to include a full justification of these so that (1) those replicating the study can understand why they have been included and (2) readers can assess the validity, reliability and generalisability of the findings that are later reported. I explain to my students that the 'why' component of the chapter is just as important as the 'what' component. The 'why' component is often poorly done in the first iteration. At best, it may be adequate in some sections but, in other sections, it may be ignored altogether. For instance, the data analysis section may fail to explain why certain data sources are appropriate for the type of data being sought to answer the research questions. Also, the selection of certain tests of statistical significance are often not justified in terms of their relevance and appropriateness.

64 Feedback on the Selection of Content

Unclear Alignment between Research Questions and Data Sources

Because the research questions are likely to be presented in a different section of the chapter to the data source information (i.e. instruments), students may fail to clearly and fully align the two. For instance, it may not be clear how one of the research questions was investigated (i.e. what data sources provided the data for answering the question). One approach that can be effective for addressing this problem is to ask students to create a table with column one stating the research questions and column two stating the data sources. Doing this makes it immediately clear if additional sources need to be considered. Once this alignment has been addressed, I ask students to create a third column between columns one and two so they can define in detail key words, constructs and terms referred to in the research questions. This exercise will often reveal a number of matters that the student has not fully considered. For example, they may not have considered how their data sources are going to provide information for all aspects of each research question. Operationalising the approach like this not only helps students to check that they have thought about the alignment, it also helps them to write this part of the chapter more clearly. An example of this approach is provided in Box 4.3.

BOX 4.3   AN EXAMPLE OF ALIGNMENT

Research questions	Definitions	Data sources
1 How do Chinese EFL teachers make their decisions about what to write and how to write it when giving EFL students feedback on their writing?	EFL = English as a foreign language Feedback = written comment on any aspect of the writing	Background interview; think-aloud protocol; retrospective interview
2 How do Chinese EFL students make their decisions about what to act on and how to act when processing their teacher's feedback?	Processing feedback = responding to the feedback given by either doing what it says or not doing what it says	Background interview; think-aloud protocol; retrospective interview

3 How effective is the communication between the teacher and the student as a result of the feedback?	Communication effectiveness = understanding by the student of what is intended by the teacher	On-going and final interviews; students' writing; student feedback and self-evaluation
4 To what extent do EFL students develop self-regulation in their writing over a semester?	Self-regulation = the ability to carry out what has been learned from the feedback on other occasions without feedback or external prompting	On-going and final interviews; students' writing; student feedback and self-evaluation

An Under-developed Data Analysis Section

Of all the sections of the methodology chapter, this tends to be the most under-developed and therefore the one that requires the most feedback. While it is understood that some details about the data analysis will be difficult to predict and will need to be added during the analysis process, most of the steps should have been considered and therefore have been described and justified in the first full version of the chapter. Typically, students fail to illustrate all the steps they followed or fail to explain what the steps produced and why. I explain that illustrations are important because they often clarify what explanations alone are unable to tell the reader. Analytical frameworks are a particularly good example of the type of illustrative detail that often needs to be provided. Examples of good practice from other dissertations can be one useful way of getting this message across.

The Findings Chapter

There are six areas in which feedback is often given on the first full iteration of the findings chapter.

Placement of Explanation and Discussion of Finding

If students are **presenting** their findings in a separate chapter to the **discussion** of their findings, they need to be clear that (a) an identification and an explanation of a finding should appear in the findings chapter and (b) a discussion of the explanation should be left to the discussion chapter. Sometimes, it is easier for readers to navigate their way through a large number of findings and

66 Feedback on the Selection of Content

discussion points if these are not in separate chapters but presented together for each research question. For example, the findings of research question 1 could be immediately followed by the discussion of these findings before the findings and discussion of research question 2 are presented. If this approach is adopted, it may be that more than one chapter is considered desirable. For instance, research questions relating to a particular theme may be presented together in one chapter while research questions relating to another theme may be presented in another chapter.

Organisation of Findings

Second, the manner in which the findings are presented needs to be logical and consistent. One form of logic typically chosen is that which presents the findings in the same order in which they are referred to in earlier chapters. For example, in some disciplines, the research questions are stated in the introduction chapter and/or in the literature review chapter(s) and there is usually a logic to how they are sequenced. Readers find it helpful if there is a consistency of approach across chapters, especially if the findings are presented according to the listed sequence and the same sequence is followed in the discussion chapter.

Hierarchical Ordering of Findings

Another organisational approach that will help readers navigate their way through the findings of a specific research question and understand their relative importance or significance to the question is one which presents the most important findings first. Giving prominence to certain findings can highlight what the student considers to be the most important questions and findings.

Tables and Figures

Tables and figures are frequently presented in a findings chapter to show the relationship between items in a table and to visually represent the tabled items in a figure. While most students are able to create tables and figures without difficulty, they may not fully appreciate the fact that the reader of their work does not have the knowledge that they have to understand detailed and/or complex tables and figures. I often find myself suggesting that two tables be created instead of one and therefore two figures (if the table is accompanied by a figure). Students will sometimes provide very little textual commentary to assist the reader's understanding of a table or figure. They may provide, for example, an introductory comment on what statistics in a table show but not add further detail to explain what they want their reader to focus on and in what order. Showing students a good example from another dissertation is one way

Feedback on the Selection of Content **67**

in which this issue can be overcome. The example of good practice presented in Box 4.4 below introduces the topic or focus of the table before inserting the table itself. This is then followed up with a textual commentary on what the student wants the reader to understand.

BOX 4.4 AN EXAMPLE OF TABLE PRESENTATION AND COMMENTARY

Table 4.1 shows the descriptive statistics for the accuracy scores in using the passive voice in the writing tasks. It indicates that the accuracy of all the three groups (DCF, ME and WP) kept improving overtime, and that the improvement is greater for the DCF group than the WP group. The somewhat high deviation in each group indicates wide variability within groups, which may limit the ability to find significance.

TABLE 4.1 Descriptive Statistics for the Scores of Accuracy in Using the Passive Voice

Group	N	Time 1		Time 2		Time 3	
		Mean	SD	Mean	SD	Mean	SD
DCF	29	37.75	30.88	48.91	31.09	54.44	33.78
ME	30	37.43	27.68	53.91	31.93	65.70	27.57
WP	28	38.16	32.86	41.26	29.85	48.64	35.19

A mixed ANOVA found a significant main effect of time averaging across the groups ($F_{(2, 168)} = 11.39$, $p < .001$, $\eta2 = .12$), but no significant main effect of group collapsing across time ($F_{(2, 84)} = 1.26$, $p = .29$, $\eta2 = .03$). Further comparison between pairs of time points indicate participants demonstrate a significant improvement in accuracy from Time1 to Time2 ($F_{(1, 84)} = 6.71$, $p = .01$, $\eta2 = .07$), from Time2 to Time3 ($F_{(1, 84)} = 4.28$, $p = .04$, $\eta2 = .05$), and from Time1 to Time3 ($F_{(1, 84)} = 25.01$, $p < .001$, $\eta2 = .23$). These indicate that all the treatment types (DCF, ME and WP) contributed to the improvement in accuracy overtime, and this is in accordance with the results of descriptive analyses reported above. The mixed ANOVA also reveals there was no significant time and group interaction ($F_{(4, 168)} = 1.02$, $p = .40$, $\eta2 = .02$), which indicates there were no significant differences in the patterns of improvement amongst the groups. In other words, no treatment type is significantly more effective than the others in producing improved accuracy in the use of the passive voice.

68 Feedback on the Selection of Content

Formatting

Sometimes students are inconsistent in the formatting of their findings. Feedback may need to draw their attention to the conventions typically used in their discipline. For example, if APA (American Psychological Association) conventions are used in the list of references, APA conventions also need to be used consistently throughout the formatting of the dissertation. Other aspects of formatting that feedback may need to be given on include the use of numbering systems. There can be a tendency for some students to present an overly detailed numbering system. This should be avoided especially when minimal content is provided in each of the sections.

The Discussion Chapter

Feedback that is typically required on the first full iteration of the discussion chapter, assuming the advice referred to in Chapter 3 has been followed, tends to be confined to (1) what the discussion points should be and (2) to the effectiveness of the links to the wider field of knowledge.

The Points of Discussion

For consistency and ease of reading, the discussion of findings needs to be set out logically and, as far as possible, structured according to the way in which the findings have been presented. Refer to the previous section on the presentation of findings where it was explained that the discussion points on each research question might (1) follow the presentation of each finding or (2) be presented in a separate discussion chapter. Sometimes, students may wish to provide a more holistic discussion of their findings in relation to an umbrella question. The more traditional approach has been to provide the more holistic type of discussion in the conclusion chapter where the student comments on the contribution of the findings to the field. However, some students may choose to provide this more overarching discussion at the end of a separate discussion of findings chapter. Feedback from supervisors is often needed on which approach is best suited to the student's work. Without this, there can be a duplication of discussion points across chapters.

Linking the Findings to the Wider Literature

There are frequently issues with the discussion of findings in light of the literature, that is, the wider picture that has been presented in the literature review. While a particular finding may be discussed in terms of several of the discourse move options, it may be that the student has not taken the discussion far enough. For example, students will often discuss the extent to which a finding corroborates or contradicts the findings of other studies but the reader may be left to ponder 'so what?' Feedback, in this situation, would do well to suggest that the student also (a) consider the theoretical literature in order to explain what the reader can understand to have been the reason for any corroboration or contradiction and (b) reflect upon the methodology used in his/her study, and that of the other studies, to see if an explanation can then be offered to explain the similarity and/or difference in findings. Additionally, supervisors may want to draw their students' attention to ways in which examples from the data may explain the findings. Having discussed each separate finding, they should ask themselves whether or not a claim can be made on the basis of their discussion points and/or whether a conclusion can be drawn. Students often struggle to take their discussion far enough and need feedback that will challenge them to consider further what they have said at certain points in their discussion.

Oral Feedback

Apart from the literature review chapter, the discussion chapter is perhaps the chapter that needs the most feedback in the latter stages of the supervisory process. Oral feedback is arguably more important than written feedback at this stage because it enables the supervisor to say more than is possible in written feedback and because it affords the opportunity for supervisors to determine, in response to points that students may make in oral meetings, where and how to challenge and/or stimulate the student's understanding about what they can say about their findings. Prior to such meetings, it may be useful to provide written feedback in the form of questions so that students have a chance to think about their responses before meeting with their supervisors. Typical questions might include the following: Why do you think this is the case? How would this be done? In what circumstances is this likely to be true? How does X relate to (compare with, support, contradict) Y? What evidence is there to support this claim or conclusion?

The Conclusion Chapter

Many of the typical sections of a conclusion chapter are handled reasonably well by students but, within each section, there may be issues that need feedback.

A Reader-friendly Summary of Findings

The conclusion will typically start with a brief overview of the aims of the study and the methodological approach that was employed in order to frame or contextualise what is said in the chapter. This is usually followed by a summary of the findings of the study. While the findings may have been summarised at various places in the findings chapter, they are often summarised in the presentation of findings chapter in terms of the type of analysis that was undertaken. For example, if the findings arose from statistical data, they are likely to have

70 Feedback on the Selection of Content

been explained in more statistical terms. In the conclusion chapter, the preferred convention is to summarise the findings for a non-expert, layman's understanding. Students often need to have their attention drawn to this expectation but once it has been pointed out, they usually manage to summarise them so that an intelligent non-specialist can understand them. The summary of findings in Box 4.5 for a dissertation research question on the effect of two types of written corrective feedback (direct error correction and the provision of meta-linguistic feedback), with and without revision, on learners' accuracy in using the English passive voice immediately after receiving the feedback and in a new text over time may not be as easily comprehended by a non-expert reader than the revised version presented in Box 4.6.

BOX 4.5 A MORE TECHNICAL SUMMARY OF FINDINGS

The findings of the between-groups analysis for RQ1 showed that all experimental groups (DC, DC+R, ME, ME+R) were effective both in the short term and in the long term. However, the DC treatment was more effective than other treatments. The results of within-groups analyses showed that all experimental groups were effective over time, but that the DC feedback group was more effective in the short term and in the long term. Thus, the DC group was more effective than other groups.

BOX 4.6 A LESS TECHNICAL SUMMARY OF FINDINGS

The findings showed that all experimental groups (direct CF, metalinguistic explanation, direct CF plus revision, meta-linguistic plus revision) outperformed the control group in both the short time and over time. However, direct CF treatment was more effective than other treatments in both the short term and over time. Additionally, the experimental groups (direct CF, meta-linguistic explanation, direct CF plus revision, meta-linguistic plus revision) significantly improved their accuracy from the pre-test to the immediate post-tests. Then, from the immediate to the delayed post-tests, the improvement deteriorated a little, but the decrease in accuracy was not significant, which reveals that the learners retained the improvement from immediate to delayed post-tests. Besides, the improved accuracy in delayed post-test was significantly higher than that in the pre-test. The results also showed that the accuracy for the control group revealed no significant differences from the pre-test to the immediate post-test and from the immediate post-test to the delayed post-test.

Making Claims and Drawing Conclusions

The conclusion chapter is all about making claims and drawing conclusions but students often need guidance about how they frame their assertions. Feedback from supervisors may need to suggest that the strength of claims and conclusions should be either hedged or boosted. It is more typically the case that students will undersell their findings and need encouragement to say that a new finding or a particularly significant finding has been revealed in their research or that a particular finding challenges earlier findings that may have claimed the opposite to the student's finding. In all situations, clear evidence and an appropriate strength of assertion is necessary. However, students often need feedback on what can be said and how it can be said. I often refer my students to Cooley and Lewkowicz (2003) where excellent guidelines on how to write claims and conclusions can be found.

Limitations

A consideration of the limitations of the student's study should include both (1) limitations in terms of any weaknesses or flaws that they have become aware of during their apprenticeship and (2) limitations in terms of the scope or parameters of the research project. Students are sometimes reluctant to be totally upfront about weaknesses or flaws in particular but it needs to be explained to them that they will be seen as more ready to do independent research if they can identify these and show that they understand the extent to which they may have negatively impacted on their findings.

Further Research

Recommendations for further research often arise out of the identified limitations but students often fail to align their limitations with recommended further research directions. If this is the case, I find it is useful for students to create a table with two columns and to identify the limitations in column one and consider whether in column two there might be suggestions that can be offered for further research.

Practice

While students usually manage to produce a range of practice applications, they are sometimes guilty of suggesting too many, including those that do not arise directly from the focus and findings of their study. Feedback on where this has occurred can usually lead to the problem being easily rectified.

72 Feedback on the Selection of Content

The Contribution of the Findings to the Field

This section, which typically comes after the summary of findings, is arguably the most important part of the dissertation because it provides the student with an opportunity to show that they understand the importance and significance of their work for the field in which it was situated. However, it can very often be a section (if included) that presents a rather superficial 'discussion' and that focuses mainly on the contribution to empirical knowledge. While the latter is certainly important, a consideration of the extent to which the research challenges, adds to or modifies existing theory is particularly important in a doctoral dissertation seeking to offer new insights and explanations about what the study explains and/or predicts. While written feedback on the other parts of the conclusion chapter tend to require little follow-up oral discussion, the contribution section almost always requires oral feedback and discussion if students are to understand and comment on the potential of their work.

The contribution to methodology is often ignored so supervisors may need to signal in their written feedback that their students should think about (1) how satisfactory their methodology was for the aims of the study and (2) whether it has provided the field with new insights and new ways of exploring the questions more fully and perhaps more robustly that earlier approaches. Feedback from supervisors might also need to focus students' attention on any aspects of their research focus that were not well investigated and therefore not well answered, (e.g. as a result of methodological shortcomings) and recommend replications or that further related studies adopt certain additional approaches.

Final Remarks

Dissertations often provide a short section called Final Remarks. It is in this section that students have the opportunity to inject a personal voice or position on their work and point to ways in which their work has opened up further research agendas. If such a closing paragraph or two has not been included, supervisors may want to suggest in their feedback that their students consider this as a positive and forward-looking way to end their work.

The Abstract

Feedback on the abstract tends to focus most often on the balance that is given to the five discourse moves identified as options in Chapter 3 (Table 3.7). Hyland (2000) refers to research that identified the various discourse move preferences found in the abstracts of different disciplines. The balance that is given to each of the moves identified across the disciplines in his book reveals that certain conventions, typically observed within one discipline, may not necessarily be the preferred conventions of other disciplines. While pre-writing advice should focus on what the supervisor and student considers relevant and important for the student's abstract, written feedback will often require suggestions about where more or less could be said about a particular discourse move. I have found that students benefit by reading Hyland's book if they need more direction in drafting their abstracts.

Having considered the advice (in Chapter 3) and the feedback (in this chapter) that supervisors may find they need to give their students on their selection of content, we can now think about what advice and feedback may need to be provided on how the content is used in the creation of argument.

5

ADVICE AND FEEDBACK ON THE CREATION OF ARGUMENT IN DISSERTATION CHAPTERS

Introduction

In Chapters 3 and 4, we considered the pre-writing advice and the post-writing feedback that supervisors typically give their doctoral students on the writing of their dissertation chapters. In this chapter, we focus on how the selected content for dissertation chapters is organised so that it serves the purpose or function(s) of the part-genre (chapter) for which it was selected. In academic genres like the dissertation, the content is organised as an 'argument' that, in one way or another, explains and develops rhetorically a case to support and justify the inclusion of the selected content. As the previous chapters explained, the nature of the content, and the argument it serves, vary from one chapter to another. Thus, the argument of a literature review, for example, is different to the argument of a results chapter. Once students and supervisors have a clear understanding of the relevant content and how it can be most effectively organised, they need to understand that the argument is only going to be rhetorically effective if there is a coherent logic to the way the content is presented. The aim of this chapter, then, is to present some pre-writing advice, in Part One, and post-writing feedback, in Part Two, that will help students to write a successful argument.

PART ONE: PRE-WRITING ADVICE

Dissertation Chapter Argument versus Textbook Content

Very often, if students are not given any pre-writing advice about what constitutes a dissertation argument, they may present, in their first draft, a catalogue of information about the area of research as one typically finds it in a textbook.

In other words, the content may not be directly related to the focus of the research (as revealed in the research questions/hypotheses). While the information selected may be relevant, students need to understand that they must use it to make an argument that is relevant to the purpose and functions of the chapter. Perhaps the best way to explain this to students is to begin with a discussion of what the term 'argument' means (see below the type of explanation that might be given) and then move on to illustrate it from an effective chapter model. Having offered this type of advice, it is useful to ask students to create a table of contents for their chapter and write a one-page outline of their argument overview (c.500–700 words) using the structure of the content in the table of contents. The more detailed the table of content is (for example, one that includes sub-headings and sub sub-headings under main headings), the more likely students are to be able to write an effective argument overview.

Understanding the Term 'Argument'

In academic writing, the term 'argument' can refer to individual claims or to the argument of a whole text (or units within a wider text). With individual claims, 'argument' refers to a proposition that is supported with evidence or reasoning, but with a whole text, it refers to 'a connected series of statements intended to establish a position and implies a response to another (or more than one) position' (Andrews, 1995, p. 3) or to 'a sequence of interlinked claims and reasons that, between them, establish content and force of the position for which a particular speaker/writer is arguing' (Toulmin, Reike & Janik, 1984, p. 14). Thus, the first defining characteristic of an argument is the development of a position. The second feature is a presentation of the position through the logical sequence of propositions that establish the position. The third characteristic of an argument is the selection of relevant information for inclusion in the development of the position. In Chapter 2, an example of an argument overview for one main section of a dissertation chapter was provided.

Understanding the Different Argument Structures of Dissertation Chapters

Drawing upon discourse moves that we referred to in Chapter 3 to understand the type of content that is relevant to each chapter or part-genre, it is useful to ask students to think about these and how they might be incorporated into the argument structure. For instance, they should think about which sub-moves might be included only once in a chapter and those that are likely to be included on more than one occasion. The following discussion of this approach, in each of the key chapters of a traditional dissertation, begins with the literature review chapter because students typically give more attention to this chapter before they write the introduction.

76 Advice/Feedback on the Creation of Arguments

The Literature Review Argument

If students consider the discourse moves of a literature review (presented earlier in Chapter 3), they will see, for example, that the first move is the establishment of 'some aspect of the knowledge territory relevant to their research' and that the sub-move options of this main move explain how this can be described and explained (i.e. by 'presenting knowledge claims and statements about theories, beliefs, constructs and definitions'). For a literature review, students are going to include more than one claim or proposition about the wider knowledge territory relevant to the focus of their dissertation. They are likely to present a number of claims or propositions for each of the content sections of the chapter. In the argument overview referred to earlier in this chapter, it can be seen that there were ten key claims or propositions about just one research question (see Box 2.10). Students who have received the advice given in Chapter 2 of this book will likely have created a mind-map that shows the relationship between key sections or topics of the literature review (i.e. by means of the main headings they have chosen) and the various claims or propositions about each section/topic (mind-map headings) so will at least have established a macro argument for their literature review. They are then in a position to consider the argument they wish to establish for the key sections of the review. In doing this, they should understand that the two main discourse moves (with their sub-move options) will be repeated a number of times. The move structure shows that once claims or propositions about an area of content knowledge have been described, explained and critiqued, where necessary, gaps in the area of knowledge can be identified and discussed in terms of their importance for investigation in the student's dissertation. Having done this for one key area or section of content, the process can be repeated for all the sections that the macro overview has identified. Once these have been presented and the gaps have been identified, main move 3 of the literature review (Table 3.2) can be presented. This move brings together the key knowledge gaps that the student has identified in the key sections of the review. From these, the research questions/hypotheses can be formulated.

The Introduction Chapter Argument

From the discourse moves identified in Chapter 3 for the introduction chapter (Table 3.1), it can be seen that the logical line of argument is given in the sequence of moves. It is often a good idea to brief students about the introductory nature of this chapter. For main moves 1 and 2, it should provide an overview of the central argument that is then more fully developed in the literature review. The third move should occupy far less space than that required for main moves 1 and 2. Typically, the third move will be covered in one or two paragraphs. I have found it is necessary to advise students to think about

Advice/Feedback on the Creation of Arguments **77**

how they are going to present their overview of the empirical and theoretical literature. For instance, they need to reflect on whether or not the focus of their research arose from a theoretical claim, position or recommendation or whether it arose from a gap in empirical knowledge. If it is the former, they should consider an outline of the theoretical case before they introduce the empirical literature related to it. However, more often than not, it is a gap in empirical knowledge that is the impetus for their research. In this case, the empirical literature should precede the theoretical explanations and predictions about the study's findings. The third option is to present one aspect of both areas of literature (e.g. a theoretical claim followed by empirical research that is related to it or a gap in the empirical literature followed by a theoretical explanation and prediction). Having this discussion with students before they write can usually reduce the amount of re-writing that is required.

The Methodology Chapter Argument

Little advice needs to be given to students about the argument structure of the methodology chapter because, unlike the literature chapter with multiple uses of certain discourse sub-moves, each of the methodology moves identified in Chapter 3 (Table 3.3) is typically presented once only and is sequenced in order of the sub-moves. That said, there are a couple of sub-moves that students tend to only cover in part. Thus, it is a good idea to advise them to make sure that their coverage of sub-move 1, about the methodological approach, explains and justifies their methodological approach from a theoretical and philosophical perspective. Readers need to know why the approach is appropriate for the focus of the research. The second additional area of advice that supervisors should provide concerns the importance of not only describing *what* was done but also *why* it was done. In this regard, it is useful to draw their attention to the fact that they can justify aspects of their methodology with reference to the literature in methodological textbooks and to why and how they were employed in other related studies, noting too that limitations and cautions identified in such studies may signal the need for future researchers to avoid or modify the approach that was used. The final piece of pre-writing advice that may be given concerns the data analysis section of the argument: advice about the importance of presenting/describing all steps in the research methodology so that a reader knows how to replicate the analysis and advice about including examples of steps taken in the analysis (e.g. illustrations from the student's data-set to explain each analytical step). Criteria frameworks are often presented to explain how each criteria was identified and categorised. Depending on the type of methodology employed in the research, some of the discourse sub-moves may be expanded while others may be conflated. Students have sometimes asked me where in the argument they would be best to present the design of their study. While disciplines may vary in the advice they give their students, I explain

78 Advice/Feedback on the Creation of Arguments

that it needs to come somewhere in the first move and maybe after sub-move (a) or built into sub-move (b). Before writing, I ask students to present me with a detailed table of contents and an argument overview of the chapter so I can see if there is a linear logic to the argument of the chapter. With their argument overview, as stated previously, it is important to see why one proposition is placed before or after another.

The Results Chapter Argument

Arguably, the presentation of results argument is the most straightforward to write, especially if it is reporting findings that arise from quantitative data. The first move, with meta-textual information (Table 3.4), is not always provided even though readers find it helpful to have this type of contextual information briefly outlined again, especially if they are reading the chapter as a stand-alone chapter at a different time to their reading of the preceding chapter. The sub-move options for main move 2 (a presentation of the results) provide a logical line of argument for each result. How each result is presented is an issue that students and supervisors need to discuss. One option is to present the findings of each research question or sub-question in the same order that they were ana-lysed. Another option is to group the findings more thematically. Before students start writing up their findings, their supervisors may want them to create a table of contents and an argument overview. However, I find that this is less necessary with this chapter as the argument structure tends not to be too complex.

The final piece of advice that is worth giving before writing commences is about the importance of not *discussing* the findings given that the chapter is only about presenting the findings. This does not mean that the findings are not *explained*. For example, explaining the relationship between points of analysis, and therefore the meaning of the relationship, is an important part of the argu-ment of the chapter. Students are often unclear about the distinction between *explanation* and *discussion* so it can be useful if the sub-moves of main move 3 for the discussion of results chapter (see Chapter 3, Table 3.5) are referred to when advice is being given.

The Discussion of Results Argument

Like the previous chapter, the discussion of results chapter may begin its argu-ment with a contextual overview. If the discussion argument is to follow the sequence of sub-moves of main move 3 (see Chapter 3, Table 3.5) as each result is presented, there is little advice that needs to be given to students before they start to write the chapter. On the other hand, if the discussion is to follow a more thematic pattern, the manner in which the argument is developed will be more complex and therefore require some advice from the supervisor. It is more likely to refer to the skills that are needed for developing a clear and logical literature review argument.

Some of the sub-move options may not be clear to students so it is advisable for supervisors to check their understanding of each move and provide advice if and where necessary. For example, the difference between making a claim based on a finding or group of findings is not necessarily the same thing as drawing a conclusion from the same findings. It is more likely that conclusions will be reached after a number of results have been referred to whereas a claim can be made about an individual result.

The Conclusion Chapter Argument

Of all the chapters where meta-text summarises key contextual information, as a reminder to readers, the conclusion chapter is possibly the one chapter where this is really not an option. My students are advised to include this because readers of a thesis will often not start at the beginning and read their way through the chapters in order of presentation. Rather, many will want to see what the study found and what the student considers the contribution of the work is to the field before they read the entire work. Others may be in search of recommendations for further research. The sequence of moves presented in Chapter 3 (Table 3.6) follows a linear logic across four main moves. Because students will sometimes fail to include all the possible recommendations for further research, they should be given advice about how additional possibilities might be thought of if they match their limitations with recommendations for further research. In thinking about this, a table comprising two columns, one for limitations and another for further research recommendations, could be created to match each limitation with a recommendation for further research.

Move 3 (about the contribution of the research to the field) tends to be the most poorly considered. It is often superficial and limited in the justifications that are offered to support the claims that are made and the conclusions that are drawn. Even when students have this explained to them, they can still fail to give this section the depth of consideration it deserves. I explain that this move is really the most important one of the whole thesis as it focuses on (a) what the study has been about, (b) what it has achieved and (c) what its contribution is likely to be to moving the field of knowledge forward. One of the best ways of helping students understand the potential of this move is to deconstruct a good model from another student's dissertation. If more than one student is preparing to write the discussion chapter, I think it is useful to bring them together for a round table discussion about what the model has achieved and how it has been attained.

The Abstract Argument

The argument of the abstract is certainly the easiest one to write. Students should be advised to follow the five main moves (see Chapter 3, Table 3.7) in sequence order and consider whether or not any of the sub-move options should not be included. They may need advice about whether, and to what

80 Advice/Feedback on the Creation of Arguments

extent, all moves should be included in the argument because dissertation abstracts can vary a lot, even within disciplines and institutions. Advice should be offered about any conventions that supervisors expect their students to follow. Compared with the dissertation chapters, where reasons are expected for everything that is stated or presented, the argument of the abstract is less about justifications and more about providing potential readers of the dissertation with an introductory overview.

PART TWO: POST-WRITING FEEDBACK

For each of the dissertation chapters, there are a number of predictable areas on which feedback may need to be given, especially about how to make the arguments more effective.

The Introduction Chapter Argument

Feedback on the argument of the introduction chapter may include the issues referred to in the earlier discussion of pre-writing advice for introduction chapters if they have not been discussed with students or if students experience difficulty in applying them. A number of additional issues may also need to be attended to by some students once their first draft of the chapter has been completed.

Defining Terms and Constructs

Sometimes students provide too much detail when defining terms and constructs that are referred to in their dissertation. In these situations, feedback needs to direct them to provide only a clear and simple, layman's type of definition at this stage but which refers the reader to the literature review chapter where a more detailed discussion of terms and constructs is presented. For instance, when researching the role of various factors in the learning of a second language (L2), researchers will need to explain what they mean by terms such as 'L2 development', 'L2 acquisition' and 'L2 learning'. In the introduction chapter, it is better to provide a simple definition of these terms and leave the wider discussion of the differences between each of them to the literature review chapter where there is space for a detailed explanation of differences as revealed in the published literature. Another term that is often referred to is 'cognitive processing'. Whole books have been devoted to descriptions and explanations of what is involved in the cognitive processing of information and the essential components of this discussion as they relate to the research focus of the dissertation are an important part of a literature review chapter, but for the introduction chapter a simple explanation that tells the reader there are a number of stages in the cognitive processing of information that need to be traversed may be sufficient at this point. As well as providing a simple working definition of terms and constructs, readers may also need to know if there are certain constraints or parameters that concern the dissertation research. For instance, the research may be more about one stage of cognitive processing, so in this situation that stage should be explained more fully than the other stages even though the other stages will need to be explained in order to provide sufficient context for the reader.

Literature Detail

Feedback often refers students to literature that is omitted or that is too extensively reported. For instance, if the dissertation research is investigating a number of variables that may have a moderating effect on the process of language learning, each of these factors needs to be clearly introduced so that the reader can understand why they might be expected to have an effect on a certain aspect of the learning process. The discussion needs to be focused though on what is necessary background for the research questions only rather than also on other ways in which such factors may play a role in the wider learning process. Getting a balance is important.

Providing the type of overview that readers need in the opening chapter can best be achieved once the literature review chapter has been completed. Students often struggle to relate the theoretical and empirical literature (a) to the problem that inspired their research and (b) to the focus of their research (as revealed by a statement of aims or a presentation of the research questions/ hypotheses). This argument focus needs to be clear and explicit. Pointing students to problems they have in achieving this may be one of the more important pieces of feedback to give them. Often, early drafts of the introduction chapter will provide more of a shopping list of sections about different theories that are considered relevant to the research question focus of the dissertation study and fail to explain the connection between the theories and research questions. In other words, there may be an absence of introductory discussion about what the theories explain and predict about the findings of the study. This is an area that I focus on strongly in oral discussion after students have drafted their proposed table of contents before writing the chapter.

Rationale and Significance of the Research

In terms of the argument logic of the chapter, an outline of the dissertation's rationale (the reasons) should either be discussed in relation to gaps in knowledge (theoretical, empirical and pedagogical) that the reader is introduced to in

82 Advice/Feedback on the Creation of Arguments

the literature background section of the chapter or be summarised at the end of this background section. Having outlined the rationale for the study, the logic of the argument can be further developed and include a brief statement about what the student believes is significant about the research that has been completed. Students often need feedback on how to link these important parts of an introduction so that each one leads logically to the next.

Occupying Their Niche

While a brief outline of the key elements of the research methodology is usually not a problem for most students, some will fail, however, to introduce their readers to a philosophical explanation of the theoretical and methodological frameworks of their research (e.g. a post-positivist explanation of why research that examines the causes of certain effects/findings is relevant and how a pre-test, treatment, post-test methodological design is then relevant to data collection). Even one or two sentences will suffice, given that a more detailed discussion of the methodological approach considered appropriate for the research focus will be provided in the literature review chapter.

Overview of the Dissertation

An overview of the structure of the dissertation is not difficult to write but many students provide little more than a 'shopping list' of what will be covered in each chapter. In doing so, they miss an opportunity to argue *why* and *how* the material they refer to is important. Feedback should draw students' attention to this if they have missed this opportunity. I encourage my students to explain what a section is going to refer to and why by means of a simple complex sentence structure (e.g. In the next section, I argue that X, because Y) or if each of the two clauses is too long, I suggest the use of two simple sentences with the first stating what the argument will focus on and the second sentence explaining why the reader needs to know this information.

The Literature Review Chapter Argument

Arguably, the literature review argument is the most difficult to write because of the amount of information that needs to be included and the complexity involved in structuring a forward-moving argument. It is likely that more iterations of this chapter's argument will be required than for those of other chapters of the dissertation. Even when clear advice is given to students before they start writing their chapter, many will struggle with the level of skill required to create a clear, logical, and rhetorically effective argument from beginning to end. So, what are the some of the key areas of feedback that supervisors will typically need to provide?

A Literature Review Argument Is Not a Shopping List of Topics Unrelated to the Focus of the Research

There is a tendency for students to present a range of literature-informed sections/topics in the first draft of their literature review that one might typically find in a book that surveys key topics related to the field. In such volumes, the topics are usually listed in some logical sequence (e.g. they might be presented according to an historical evolution or they may be organised according to theoretical sections that are followed by research sections or according to general themes before more specific themes). In a dissertation, however, the content needs to be organised in such a way that it relates directly to the argument that the student is presenting. Thus, feedback will often need to draw students' attention to the importance of (a) arguing why and how the literature, that has been selected, is relevant to and explicitly informs the case being developed around the various foci of the dissertation and (b) ensuring that one proposition/claim/argument leads to and informs the next. Feedback will often need to direct students to places in the review where the argument is either not evident or is not logically informed by what precedes or follows it.

The Literature Has Not Been Critically Evaluated

Some students experience a lot of difficulty with critically assessing (a) the quality of different claims and conclusions reported in the literature and (b) the validity, reliability, robustness of empirical research and the claims/conclusions it has led to. Assessing both of these aspects is not easy. Many students will simply provide a descriptive outline of different theoretical positions and different research findings and not critically evaluate them or use them for the purposes of arguing a proposition. Students sometimes need to be given feedback on the importance of explaining/justifying why they have adopted a particular perspective or position. In other words, they may need to be alerted to the importance of taking a position and justifying it in relation to the focus of their research. For instance, when discussing the various theoretical perspectives that are potentially relevant to the focus of the dissertation research, students need to identify these perspectives and explain why they have situated their research focus within only one or some of these. The discussion needs to explain the choice insofar as it is the most appropriate for the specific focus of the research questions. Additionally, feedback sometimes needs to be given to students about not being overly selective in which theoretical literature they choose to present, hoping that the examiner or readers in general are not aware of the potential relevance of other theoretical perspectives.

The Methodology Chapter Argument

While some students need feedback on the key areas that should be presented in the methodology chapter, few need much feedback on the argument structure of the chapter.

84 Advice/Feedback on the Creation of Arguments

The 'Why' as well as the 'What'

Once students have covered the 'what' aspects of the chapter, they need to also realise that a doctoral dissertation requires a consideration of 'why' each aspect was chosen. Feedback on the need for justification may only need to be provided in certain parts of the chapter. They sometimes need feedback on the importance of explaining why one of two equally relevant approaches was adopted in the methodology and why the second of the two was not selected (e.g. why interviews were included instead of survey questionnaires). The feedback, in this case, may need to direct students to a consideration of the instrument best able to provide the data that are relevant to the central focus of a research question. Thus, students may need to have their attention drawn to the importance of justifying their descriptive 'what' details in the argument structure of the chapter. On some occasions, when the 'why' component of the argument has been presented, feedback may need to point out that the justification is under-developed or not well related to the 'what' component. Another aspect of the methodology that sometimes need supervisor feedback is the choice of analytical framework employed in the research. Not only does this chapter need to describe in careful detail the various component parts of the framework, it also needs to explain what these parts contribute to the analysis and why.

Procedural Gaps in the Argument

It is very easy for students, in knowing the detail about the processes and procedures they included in their methodology, to forget to mention a critical procedure that enabled them to move from one step to another. Feedback may need to remind them of the importance of presenting every step they followed so that any reader who wants to replicate the study can do so by following what has been presented in the chapter. The section of the chapter that tends to need more feedback in this regard is the data analysis section. Very often students will state that table X, figure X or framework X itemises and illustrates the steps that were taken in a certain part of their data analysis but forget that readers may not know which part of the table/figure/framework they need to focus on first. Thus, feedback may need to direct students to the absence of textual explanation about how to follow or read the tables, figures and frameworks. Another part of the methodology chapter that supervisors may need to provide feedback on is the data collection process. This is particularly important if data have been collected from a range of sources and instruments and at different times. Suggesting that students present all this information in a table that identifies the sequence of each step in the collection process is one effective way of helping to eliminate the omission of key information. Once the table been created, the accompanying text is likely to be more complete.

The Presentation of Results Chapter Argument

Once a decision has been made about the macro structure of the chapter (e.g. presenting findings for each research question/hypothesis according to the order in which they were investigated), students tend to have few difficulties with the argument structure of their content. That said, two easily resolved issues may occasionally present themselves in an early draft of the chapter's argument.

Not Distinguishing between an Explanation and a Discussion

Sometimes, an explanation about what a group of findings means, including, for example, an explanation about what the numbers in a table mean, may suddenly become a point of discussion. If the presentation and discussion of findings are being presented in the same chapter, this is not an issue, but in dissertations where a clear demarcation has been identified in the introduction chapter's outline of the content of other chapters this becomes an issue that feedback needs to point to. Sometimes, as mentioned earlier, students simply confuse the two words 'explanation' and 'discussion'. For instance, pointing to patterns in the findings of a research question is not a discussion. Explaining why the patterns occurred as they did would be a discussion of possible reasons.

Layman's Explanation versus Methodological/Technical Explanation

Typically a presentation of findings involves the use of technical terms associated with the analysis process. This is not a problem but students sometimes need to be reminded that, at the end of each finding, it is expected that there will be an explanation of the finding in layman's terms so it is clear what it reveals about one of the research questions. An example of the difference between the two types of reporting is presented below in the section on the conclusion chapter argument. Sometimes students have difficulty making this transition because they have become so immersed in the analytical process that they struggle to explain the finding in terms that an intelligent non-expert will understand. This final step in the presentation of a finding is an important component of the argument structure of the chapter and examiners will want to see that students are able to explain their work with and without technical terminology.

The Discussion of Results Chapter Argument

Like the argument structure of the literature review chapter, the argument of the discussion of results chapter can also present students with challenges even if they take on board the discourse move options outlined in Chapter 3.

86 Advice/Feedback on the Creation of Arguments

Not Taking a Point of Discussion Far Enough

The range of sub-moves (for main move 3) identified as options for expanding the discussion of a particular finding follow a logical sequence that students can follow when deciding how to argue their discussion points (Table 3.5). On some occasions, a finding may not warrant such an extensive discussion but supervisory feedback should suggest that students consider each option and eliminate those that, after reflection, would not add anything to their argument. In several respects, students may fail to take the discussion of their findings as far as they can. For example, they may only give a partial explanation for why a finding occurred as it did (i.e. whether it met expectations or failed to meet expectations). Feedback may need to encourage the student to consider more fully the reasons for a particular finding occurring as it did (e.g. by comparing the methodology of their study with those of other studies where differences in variables may have been a primary reason for any difference in findings). For example, students sometimes suggest that other studies have reported that a particular finding occurred because a certain variable was present and therefore had an effect on the finding but they fail to explain why the presence of that variable in their own study had a similar effect. In other words, they may fail to adequately explain why the same factor may have had a similar effect in the two studies. Students are frequently slow to think about what the theoretical literature can offer by way of explanation. Additionally, students are sometimes satisfied if they can suggest one explanation for a findings and may need to be prompted to consider the influence or interacting effect of other factors or variables. Then, at the end of their discussion, there may be an opportunity for them to make a claim or draw a conclusion about the finding that they have been discussing (e.g. about the generalisability of the finding to other contexts). It may be necessary to draw their attention to this additional point of discussion.

Not Discussing Findings in Relation to the Wider Picture

Many students focus only on the published research findings when explaining why their findings occurred as they did. If they do this, feedback needs to remind them, as mentioned above, that reasons (the 'why' factors) can also be drawn from the theoretical literature. The argument in the discussion chapter needs to be developed so that it is clear what the students' findings have contributed to the wider field of knowledge. It is this aspect of the discussion that some students are shy to engage with, either because it requires a higher level of engagement and reflection than they may want to commit to or because they feel their work is too limited in scope to have a significant impact beyond the confines of their own study. Sometimes students think that if they do some 'name-dropping' of other studies/authors, that will be all that is needed. Supervisors may need to point out that that is only the starting point. Explaining the connection between one's own findings and the knowledge already established in the field is arguably the most important part of any discussion of findings.

The Conclusion Chapter Argument

If students follow the discourse move structure of a conclusion chapter, referred to in Chapter 3 (Table 3.6), they will know that there is a logic to the rhetorical sequencing of the various sections. Nevertheless, feedback is sometimes required on some of the sections.

Summary of Findings

Because the conclusion chapter is sometimes read before other chapters, the summary of findings needs to be written in non-technical language and be directly explained in terms of the aims or research questions/hypotheses. As I mentioned earlier, students may need to have their attention drawn to places in this section where this clarity and explicitness has not been provided.

Contribution to the Field of Knowledge

In many respects, this is the most important part of the dissertation because it is here that students show an understanding of what their work has achieved and what it adds to the body of knowledge. The argument it presents, in this regard, needs to be carefully organised and carefully explained/justified. Sometimes, students need feedback on where their argument is weak (e.g. is not organised, is not well justified, is under-developed in terms of explaining its contribution to theory-building, new empirical knowledge, and new methodological approaches). In particular, while students can usually see clearly and explain clearly what their findings have contributed as new empirical knowledge, they sometimes struggle to use this as a platform from which to argue their contribution to theory-building (e.g. the extent to which their work corroborates existing theoretical explanations and predictions, the extent to which it suggests that additions be made to existing theoretical perspectives or the extent to which it challenges some aspect of existing theory). Feedback is also needed to guide students in their thinking about the extent to which the methodology used in their studies revealed (a) the effectiveness of a particular approach that had not been considered in earlier research for investigating a particular type of research focus or question or (b) the need for additional approaches that might better facilitate, for example, more robust findings. Having argued the contribution to these three areas, students usually do not have too much difficulty suggesting a range of practice applications. However, feedback may need to point out where the suggestions are outside the scope of the study or have not been specifically derived from the findings of the study.

Limitations

Limitations can refer to the scope or parameters of a study as well as to any weaknesses or shortcomings in a study. Several areas of feedback may need to be provided in relation to this section. Students usually understand the need to refer to the latter even though they may be reluctant to identify too many of these in case they 'shoot themselves in the foot' and undermine what they may have said about the contribution of their work to the field. Feedback is typically needed on the extent to which their work may have been compromised in some way as a result of any limitations they were working within.

The Abstract Argument

The constraints associated with the need for brevity can mean that feedback may sometimes be required.

Length of the Abstract

Most supervisors suggest that the abstract should not be longer than 1–1.5 pages of the dissertation. Feedback may need to be given on which of the five main moves can be edited, if necessary (Table 3.7). For example, some disciplines ignore the fifth move altogether and focus primarily on moves 2–4 (the aims of the research, the methodology and the key findings).

Alignment of Aims/Research Questions and Range of Findings

If there are a number of supporting or operational research questions, for example, these may need to be reduced to two or three of the main aims/research questions. This, in turn, may mean that feedback needs to be given on (a) the range of findings identified in the abstract and (b) the inclusion of those that directly align with the aims/questions that have been identified.

This chapter has sought to identify the key areas of advice and feedback that supervisors believe their students will benefit from when creating an argument from the content they have selected. The next chapter focuses on feedback that may be required to help them write more coherent arguments.

6

ADVICE OR FEEDBACK ON THE COHERENCE OF DISSERTATION ARGUMENTS

Introduction

The content of this chapter may be considered either as advice to give students before they start writing their chapters or as areas of feedback that often need to be addressed once the draft of a chapter has been submitted. Over the years, I have tended to focus more on coherence issues once I see the type of argument my students produce. Thus, the focus is more on feedback. Nevertheless, I do always alert them to the importance of creating coherent text when advice is given about the content and argument structure of a chapter before they turn their table of contents into text.

Coherent writing is essential if an argument is to be clearly and logically developed and soundly justified. However, little has been written about how supervisors and others address incoherent writing. This lacuna may be the result of a lack of understanding about (a) what constitutes coherent text and (b) how to explicitly articulate what is expected. Dictionaries of terms and concepts, like that compiled by Finch (2000) for example, can offer a variety of guidelines on some of the characteristics of a coherent argument. They refer to coherence in terms of cohesion and clearly organised ideas, an uninterrupted connection or unity of ideas, and comprehensible language or thought. Achieving a coherent argument is something that many students experience a degree of difficulty with. As a result, supervisors often find it necessary to provide feedback on what can be done to make a text more coherent. In this chapter, some of the areas of feedback that may be provided to address weaknesses in the coherence of dissertation arguments are identified: at the macro level, within a section, within a

90 Advice/Feedback on Coherence of Arguments

paragraph and within a sentence. Some supervisors may choose to present this material as pre-writing advice rather than use it only to guide them when it comes to giving feedback.

Coherence at the Macro Level

Students sometimes need feedback on the need for clearer wording in the headings of major sections of a chapter so that the focus of the section is more readily apparent to the reader. They should be encouraged to ask themselves if the words they have chosen are appropriate and sufficient to reveal the focus of their arguments. Consider, for example, the difference between Examples 1 and 2 in Box 6.1 where it can be seen that the first heading, in Example 1, while telling the reader that the section will be about different types of written corrective feedback, does not provide the same level of information about the section that Example 2 does. The challenge is always to make a heading as short as possible but, at the same time, to make it as informative as possible about the focus of the section.

BOX 6.1

Example 1

Different types of written corrective feedback

Example 2

Are some types of written corrective feedback more effective than others for language learning?

Having read the heading given to a major section of a chapter, an advance organiser that outlines briefly the argument of the section can then be very helpful for the reader, especially if the section contains a range of topics. Advance organisers can simply outline the key areas of focus or they can go one step further and provide an argument that explains why the chosen areas of focus are relevant to the section and to the aims of the dissertation research. It may be useful to show students an example of both of the approaches so they can see how an example that goes a step further is more suitable for a doctoral dissertation (i.e. where both the 'what' and the 'why' components of the argument overview are outlined). Example 3 in Box 6.2 illustrates how attention has been given to both components.

BOX 6.2

Example 3

The assumption behind this question is that certain types of written corrective feedback may be more effective than others in facilitating second language development. As a result, it has led to a plethora of studies over the decades. However, in spite of the investigations, a number of teachers and researchers continue to say that they do not have a clear answer to the question. The aim of this section, then, is (1) to consider the studies that have specifically focused on the relative effectiveness of different types of written corrective feedback on the output that learners produce and see what conclusions their authors draw and (2) to consider the extent to which an overall answer can be given to the question.

Sub-sections of a major section also require appropriate and sufficient wording to make their focus clear. The use of a numbering system can also add clarity. Example 4 in Box 6.3 is an effective illustration of how this can be done for several sub-sections in a main section.

BOX 6.3

Example 4

1.1 Are some types of written corrective feedback more effective than others for second language development?

    1.1.1   the effectiveness of direct written corrective feedback

           1.1.1.1   studies before 1996

           1.1.1.2   studies since 1996

    1.1.2   the effectiveness of indirect written corrective feedback

    1.1.3   the effectiveness of meta-linguistic written corrective feedback

It can be seen in this example that the numbering system clarifies the hierarchical role of the different sub-headings of the argument.

Finally, a summary or a final sentence in a major section can inform the reader about what is to follow in the next section and why, thereby signalling the logic of the argument's development. Example 5 in Box 6.4 illustrates how this may be achieved.

92 Advice/Feedback on Coherence of Arguments

BOX 6.4

Example 5

In conclusion, it is clear from the findings reported in this section that it is not possible to reach a single answer about whether one type of written corrective feedback can be expected to be more or less effective than another type because the interactional effect of the different types of feedback with other variables signals a need to consider the potential effect of these factors with feedback types on language development.

The concluding sentence in this example indicates that the next section of the chapter will focus on other factors or variables that might have an interactional and moderating effect with different types of written corrective feedback on language development.

Coherence within a Section

Coherence within a major section is not always easily achieved by some students, especially the type of coherence that is needed to tie all aspects of content to the line of argument being developed in the section. However, if the same types of approach, as described above, are followed, students should be able to establish a coherent argument. Appropriate and sufficient wording in sub-section headings and the use of further sub-headings within sub-sections, the inclusion of a short advance organiser (e.g. one or two sentences) and clear numbering of sections can work together to reveal the direction of an argument. Additionally, attention should also be given to establishing links between sub-sections and between paragraphs. Clear topic sentences at the beginning of sub-sections and paragraphs can signal, at the outset, the focus of sub-sections and paragraphs within sub-sections. Example 6 in Box 6.5 illustrates how this may be achieved.

BOX 6.5

Example 6

There are several reasons for focusing on the potential role of written corrective feedback to help second language learners of English overcome errors in their use of the English article system.

This topic sentence clearly introduces the reader to the focus of the section that it introduces (i.e. the focus on reasons for the claim that is made).

The topic sentence, of Example 7 in Box 6.6, that follows this discussion of reasons introduces the reader to a more detailed consideration of the first reason identified in the paragraph.

BOX 6.6

Example 7

An accurate use of the article system can be problematic for second language learners from certain first language backgrounds where the article system is not observed.

Similarly, the final sentence of a sub-section and a paragraph that concludes a section or a paragraph and that points to the focus of the next sub-section or paragraph are two strategies that can aid the cohesion and coherence of an argument. In the discourse literature, these are sometimes referred to as transitions. Example 8 in Box 6.7 illustrates how this may be achieved.

BOX 6.7

Example 8

While this section has shown that there are a number of stages in the cognitive processing of new linguistic knowledge, the extent to which the second language proficiency level of a learner may moderate the effectiveness of this cognitive processing from stage to stage needs to now be considered.

It can be seen that this concluding sentence operates as a transition between what has just been discussed (the fact that there are different stages of cognitive processing) and what is to be discussed next (the extent to which language learners' proficiency in using the target language may influence their processing, from one stage to another).

Coherence within a Paragraph

Many students need feedback on the coherence of the argument presented within a paragraph. If each paragraph signals clearly its central focus early in

94 Advice/Feedback on Coherence of Arguments

the paragraph (and this can be achieved if the approaches just described are followed) and all sentences that follow describe, explain or illustrate the central idea of the paragraph, there is a greater likelihood of the paragraph achieving coherence than if it doesn't. The paragraph in Example 9 of Box 6.8 illustrates how this may be done.

BOX 6.8

Example 9

Truscott (1996) argued that there was no evidence from the published research available at the time he was writing to support the view that written corrective feedback has the potential to facilitate second language development. However, his claims in relation to each of the four studies he cited as evidence (Kepner, 1991; Robb et al., 1986; Semke, 1984; Sheppard, 1992) have been critiqued on the grounds that each study contained sufficient research design flaws to mean that the findings and the claims may be invalid and/or unreliable. In all four studies, it has been noted that there was an absence of a control group and that the accuracy performance of the participants could therefore not be measured against that of learners who received written corrective feedback. However, some have argued that learners who received content-related comments can be compared with learners who received written corrective feedback because the content comments may not have included any reference to accuracy or form. Nevertheless, those who maintain that a control group must not receive any type of feedback (content comments included) caution against the conclusions drawn by the researchers and by Truscott. Other flaws or shortcomings in these studies have been identified and are discussed in the following paragraphs.

It can be seen from the opening sentence of this paragraph that the topic of the paragraph is about whether or not written corrective feedback has the potential to facilitate second language development. This opening is developed with the first of several arguments in support of claims about whether or not written corrective feedback can facilitate language development: Truscott's argument against the potential of the practice and the empirical studies he refers to as evidence; counter arguments from others who draw attention to the fact that, on one count at least (i.e. the absence of a control group in the design of the studies), the claim is flawed. The argument ends by stating that there are additional arguments that can be levelled against Truscott's claim and that these will be followed up in the following paragraphs.

Advice/Feedback on Coherence of Arguments **95**

In paragraphs where a number of reasons may be given to support a claim or a proposition that is introduced in the topic sentence of a paragraph, discourse markers (such as 'first' or 'firstly', 'second' or 'secondly' and so on) can visually highlight and separate one reason from another as we can see in Example 10 of Box 6.9.

BOX 6.9

Example 10

On three grounds, Truscott (1996) argues that written corrective feedback cannot be expected to help second language learners acquire target-like proficiency in their use of the target language. First, he claims that there are theoretical reasons against the practice. Second, he argues that there is no empirical evidence to support the view that error correction is helpful for learners. Third, he suggests that teachers are often unable or ill-equipped to provide helpful feedback.

Other discourse markers or connectors can be used to signal different relationships between sentence ideas. The three most commonly used ones include 'addition' or 'also', 'contrast' or 'however', and 'result' or 'therefore'. Others that may be used include 'nevertheless', 'moreover', 'consequently', 'besides' and 'furthermore'. While these may highlight a particular relationship between sentence ideas, they can also be over-used or used incorrectly by some students. Often these connectors are used at the beginning of a sentence even though this is not the only position in a sentence where they may be used to good effect. As an illustration, Example 11 in Box 6.10 highlights the markers in bold.

BOX 6.10

Example 11

In order to explain their empirical findings on the benefits of written corrective feedback, researchers often draw upon selective aspects of SLA theory. Apart from a rather piecemeal approach to understanding why written corrective feedback is effective for some learners and not others, little attention has been given in the literature to an overall argument that explains how and why learners make (or fail to make) effective use of the feedback for their second language development, both immediately and over time.

(Continued)

96 Advice/Feedback on Coherence of Arguments

(Continued)

By comparison, more attention has been given to understanding how and why learners develop their knowledge through oral interaction and feedback. This is understandable because spontaneous oral language is most often considered a better approximation of second language competence. **Nevertheless**, in recent years, a number of articles and books have identified some of the ways in which SLA theory-building in the oral context may also have something to say about how and why written corrective feedback may contribute to second language development. **However**, the insights from these reflections have not been sufficiently developed in the form of an overall theoretical argument or model to explain the potential contribution of written corrective feedback for second language development. The purpose of this paper, **then**, is to present an argument that builds on these. **Consequently**, it draws upon two of the dominant theoretical traditions in the SLA literature.

While the judicious use of discourse markers can contribute to the clarity and, therefore, to the coherence of an argument within a paragraph, students should be advised to focus their efforts on creating relationships as much as possible between ideas and propositions (e.g. by focusing on the meaning connections of ideas across sentences). If this approach is encouraged, the frequency with which readers need to fill the meaning gap between one sentence and another sentence will be reduced. Supervisors often find themselves asking their students what the connection is between two sentences, that is, how one sentence leads to the next in terms of meaning and logic. Example 12, in Box 6.11, illustrates the problem while Example 13 in Box 6.11 also illustrates how it may be resolved. Example 13 illustrates how sentence 3 is required between sentence 1 and sentence 2 in Example 12 if the reader is to understand the connection between them. If sentence 3 had been placed between sentences 1 and 2 in example 12, the reader would have understood why sentence 2 referred to the interface position.

BOX 6.11

Example 12

Sentence 1

Krashen argues that, because two types of knowledge are located in separate parts of the brain, explicit knowledge cannot be converted to implicit knowledge.

Sentence 2

On the other hand, the interface position argues that conversion is possible.

Example 13

Sentence 3

This position is known as the non-interface position.

Coherence within a Sentence

Comprehensible language is critical to coherence at the sentence level. Thus, it is not surprising that supervisors often need to suggest in their feedback that the choice of vocabulary and/or syntax needs to be reconsidered. Choosing the imprecise or wrong word can render a sentence incoherent. Sometimes the word that should have been chosen can be deduced from the context but this is not always possible. Choosing the precise word to convey an intended meaning is critical when claims are made or conclusions are drawn about the work or ideas of other people. The choice of verb, for example, to signal one's position in relation to a claim or conclusion is essential for accurate communication. The difference in meaning between the words 'suggesting', 'asserting' and 'admitted' or between 'said', 'claimed', 'stated' and 'admitted' is sufficient to signal an unintended meaning if the incorrect verb is used. As a result, the coherence of the argument can be affected if students are unaware of the different positions or stances each of these verbs signal. In Examples 14 and 15 of Box 6.12 there is an important difference between the stance of the author in Example 14 and that of the author in Example 15. The verb **argues** conveys the idea that Truscott has argued a claim with a number of reasons and supportive evidence whereas the verb **states** indicates that he has only mentioned the claim but not necessarily argued a case for it.

BOX 6.12

Example 14

Truscott (1996) **argues** that written corrective feedback is ineffective as a pedagogical practice.

Example 15

Truscott (1996) **states** that written corrective feedback is ineffective as a pedagogical practice.

98 Advice/Feedback on Coherence of Arguments

Sometimes an incorrect tense can suggest that an action took place once and once only in the past rather than as an on-going action in the past. Other instances of a faulty use of tenses can be found in Cooley and Lewkowicz (2003). It is important that students receive feedback on the uses of different tenses so that they convey exactly when an action was done, is continuing to be done or will be done. The following advice in Box 6.13 may be useful as a guide.

BOX 6.13   THE USE OF VERB TENSES

Tense	Use
Past simple	To refer to what has been done
Past and present simple	To refer to what was written in a paper, rather than what was done, is being referred to
Present simple	To refer to the currency of a debate
Present perfect	To refer to a whole area of study before individual examples of studies within the area are described in the past or present simple
Present perfect	To refer to the currently accepted state of knowledge being different to what was previously accepted

---

Inaccurate syntax and overly long sentences can often render a sentence incoherent. Any form of grammatical error can have an effect on the coherence of a sentence. Inaccurate clause structures can mean that the relationship between one clause and another is unclear as Example 16 in Box 6.14 illustrates.

BOX 6.14

Example 16

Individual and contextual factors that can moderate the cognitive processing of written corrective feedback information may be categorised as internal cognitive factors, for example, the learner's working memory and the learner's processing capacity, as internal motivational/affective factors, for example, the learner's goals, interests, attitudes, interests and beliefs, and as external factors, for example, the complexity and the distributional characteristics of the input, the learning context and social factors.

The main problem with Example 16 is the faulty punctuation. As a result, the clause structure of the text becomes unclear. However, as a re-working of the sentence in Example 17 of Box 6.15 reveals, it is possible to make the sentence more coherent for the reader even though a listing of the factor categories would provide an even more coherent statement.

BOX 6.15

Example 17

Individual and contextual factors that can moderate the cognitive processing of written corrective feedback information may be categorised as internal cognitive factors (e.g. the learner's working memory and the learner's processing capacity), as internal motivational/affective factors (e.g. the learner's goals, interests, attitudes, interests and beliefs) and as external factors (e.g. the complexity and the distributional characteristics of the input, the learning context and social factors).

Overly long sentences can sometimes appear, on a single reading, to be incoherent even if their grammatical forms and structures are accurately formed. For instance, if a sentence contains more than three clauses, the relationship between all of the clauses can be unclear if the reader is unaccustomed to retaining so much information. The sentence in Example 18 of Box 6.16 illustrates this problem and the need for the sentence to be divided into more than one sentence as Example 19 in Box 6.17 illustrates.

BOX 6.16

Example 18

Adding to our understanding of the specific cognitive processes and conditions involved in processing from one stage to the next is McLaughlin's Information Processing Model which draws on insights about information processing from cognitive psychology and which posits the view that learners are limited in how much information they are able to consciously process at any one time because of the nature and complexity of the oral or written task/activity they are performing and their own information processing capacity.

BOX 6.17

Example 19

Adding to our understanding of the specific cognitive processes and conditions involved in processing from one stage to the next is McLaughlin's Information Processing Model. This model draws on insights about information processing from cognitive psychology. It posits the view that learners are limited in how much information they are able to consciously process at any one time because of (1) the nature and complexity of the oral or written task/activity they are performing and (2) their own information processing capacity.

It can be seen that the use of three sentences is more reader-friendly than the single sentence of Example 18. The addition of (1) and (2) in the third sentence of Example 19 further highlights the two reasons that are given and further adds to the coherence of the statement.

This brings to a close the advice and feedback that supervisors might find useful when helping their students overcome some of the common writing difficulties or issues they may encounter during their dissertation journey. In the next chapter, I provide guidelines that may be presented as advice or feedback to students who undertake other forms of academic writing related to what they are presenting in their dissertations.

7

ADVICE AND FEEDBACK ON THE WRITING OF OTHER TEXTS DURING THE DISSERTATION JOURNEY

Introduction

During the doctoral supervision period, most students want to present something from their research at either a national or international conference. This, of course, is to be encouraged because it exposes them to feedback on their work from those outside the supervisory team. Supervisors will typically provide their students with some advice on (a) what is expected by a conference abstract reviewing committee, (b) the construction of PowerPoint slides for the oral presentation and (c) the writing of a conference paper or a journal article. In this chapter, I offer some advice on writing the conference abstract in Part One, on preparing the PowerPoint slides in Part Two and on writing a journal article in Part Three.

PART ONE: WRITING A CONFERENCE ABSTRACT

There is an art to writing an effective conference abstract. The following advice touches on some of the most important factors for consideration but it does not pretend to be an exhaustive list of criteria as these can vary from conference to conference. Some conference websites provide a list of the key criteria that the review committee will use when selecting abstracts for inclusion in the conference programme. It is useful to discuss with students the type of information they can expect to find on conference websites. In Box 7.1, for example, the American Association for Applied Linguistics (AAAL) provides information on various topics.

102 Advice/Feedback on the Writing of Other Texts

BOX 7.1 GUIDELINES ON THE AAAL WEBSITE

1 Strands
2 Proposals

    a) Individual papers
    b) Posters
    c) Roundtable discussions
    d) Colloquia
    e) Shorter paper sessions
    f) Audio visual (AV) equipment

3 Proposal format
4 Evaluation of proposals
5 AAAL proposal policies
6 Submission process
7 Requests for meeting spaces
8 Questions

In preparing to write an abstract, students should seek as much information as possible about how the abstract will be evaluated. In this regard, the information (in Box 7.2) provided on the AAAL website is very useful.

BOX 7.2 AAAL ABSTRACT CRITERIA FOR ACCEPTANCE

Proposals for individual papers, posters and roundtable sessions are evaluated by a team of reviewers according to each of the following categories:

- Appropriateness and significance of the topic/issue/problem
- Expectation of original research
- Research design if an empirical study, including clearly stated questions, data sources, data collection procedures, and analytic approach
- Conceptual framework if a conceptual study, including integration of topic into current thinking, clear exposition of treatment of topic and contributions to the literature
- Manner of presentation (indicative of a clear and well-organised presentation)

Advice/Feedback on the Writing of Other Texts **103**

In broad terms, these criteria align with what has been published in the literature about the key characteristics of an abstract for a dissertation. However, it useful to have a discussion with students about which of the discourse move characteristics in Box 7.3 are also typically included in a conference abstract. The reason for drawing the attention of students to this is that the aim of a conference abstract is, to some extent, different to that of a dissertation abstract. The following discourse moves typically considered by students and academics when writing an abstract for a dissertation or journal article should perhaps be discussed first.

BOX 7.3 DISCOURSE MOVE OPTIONS FOR THE WRITING OF A DISSERTATION OR JOURNAL ARTICLE ABSTRACT

Main moves	Sub-moves
Introduction	Establish context of the paper and what motivated the research or discussion
Purpose	Indicate purpose, thesis or hypothesis and outline the intention behind the paper
Method	Provide information on design, procedures, assumptions, approach, data, etc.
Product	State main findings or results, the argument, or what was accomplished
Conclusion	Interpret or extend results beyond scope of paper, draw inferences, point to applications or wider implication

---

Having discussed these characteristics, supervisors can then explain what sets the dissertation or article abstract apart from the conference abstract. In this discussion, it is important to point out that the conference abstract is written for conference delegates who want to know whether or not they should attend the presentation. In this respect, then, it is more of a promotional document and, as such, should not outline all the key findings or conclusions that will be delivered in the presentation. On the other hand, in the dissertation abstract, the key findings and some conclusions are certainly provided.

Another difference between the two types of abstract can be the choice of language used. In the conference abstract, more colourful or persuasive language may be used, whereas in the dissertation abstract the language tends to align more with the type of plain English that might be expected in a report. It should also be explained that some conference committees ask for

104 Advice/Feedback on the Writing of Other Texts

an abstract that contains 300 or 500 words but that they only publish in the conference handbook or on the conference website a summary version of the abstract. The reason for this is that the committee wishes to see whether or not the content of the presentation is likely to be relevant to and of sufficient quality for the conference.

Having had this discussion, it may be useful to discuss a deconstruction of a conference abstract. In Box 7.4, an example is presented of an abstract that was considered effective by a conference review team.

BOX 7.4 AN EXAMPLE OF A SUCCESSFUL CONFERENCE ABSTRACT

In recent years, a number of studies have reported the value of written CF for the development of certain linguistic forms and structures but only a few case studies have begun to investigate whether certain individual and contextual factors are more likely than others to moderate the types of response of learners to written CF and the cognitive processing of such input. This presentation will report on a study of 45 advanced EAP students in a large university in X. Of the three groups formed, one received indirect written CF on the targeted grammatical errors (definite and indefinite articles) made in a pre-test text, the second received written meta-linguistic information about the errors they had made and the third was a control group. A short questionnaire was administered immediately after the pre-test to investigate what the learners thought about the task they had just completed. One week later, those in the first two groups received written CF on the errors they had made and were given five minutes to look over their corrected texts before they wrote a new text. Both texts were of the compare and contrast genre. After writing task two, they were given a more extensive questionnaire that elicited how and why they thought they had responded to the feedback in the way they had done. Findings will be reported on (1) the range of responses about writing task one; (2) the nature of and reasons for their responses to the feedback and its impact on their writing of task two; (3) the relationship between (1) and (2) on whether uptake occurred and whether or not there was an additional effect for feedback type and error categories.

It can be seen that this promotional abstract focused on the nature of the study and outlined the focus of the findings as a tease about what to expect at the presentation. Some conference committees require that references be included in the abstract while others specifically state that they should not be provided. The abstract above specifically stated that references should not to be included.

Having completed the abstract and been advised that it has been accepted for inclusion in the conference programme, it is time to think about the content of the PowerPoint slides.

PART TWO: THE CONSTRUCTION OF POWERPOINT SLIDES FOR A CONFERENCE PRESENTATION

A number of factors need to be understood by students before they start creating their slides.

The Number of Slides

The presentation slot will typically be 20 minutes with 5–10 minutes for questions and discussion. This means that an assessment needs to be made about the number of slides that can be included. As a guide only, I would suggest no more than one per minute. It is important to point out to students that conference presentations are usually about work that has not been published and that, if the focus is an empirical piece of research, the audience will be most interested in the research and less interested in the literature background.

The Content of Each Slide

It is important that PowerPoint slides are clear and uncluttered. Slides that include numbered or bullet-point notes are preferable to those that include complete sentences because the latter has the tendency to mean that presenters will have difficulty engaging with their audience if they need to read sentences. On average, four ideas or points should be enough content and this may include a couple of subsidiary points. Providing a title for each slide can help the listener keep track of the key points in the argument being presented.

The Design of Each Slide

The size of lettering and choice of fonts need to be considered carefully so that members of the audience at the back of the presentation room can see everything that is on each slide. Diagrams, figures and tables need to be set out in a clear manner so that the audience can follow what is being said and where the presenter is up to on each slide. When speaking about this type of slide, the logic of the slide's message needs to be readily apparent. For instance, the use of columns and rows, and the use of arrows, for example, can provide visual clarity. Having thought about these characteristics of PowerPoint slides, advice needs to be given about how to decide what content to present.

106 Advice/Feedback on the Writing of Other Texts

The Focus of the Presentation

Because the abstract has been written, the focus of the presentation will have been decided. However, apart from the title slide (which should align with the title of the presentation submitted and accepted by the conference committee), a decision needs to be made about the overall direction of the presentation. Thus, a summary outline of the topics of the key slides should be considered even though these may, to some extent, change as the slides are being created. For example, the summary outline slide might be called *An outline of the presentation* or *The roadmap for the talk*.

Statement of Aims, Research Questions/Hypotheses

This slide can provide a list of the aims, questions or hypotheses that guided the research to be reported. Sometimes, if some of the key words or constructs referred to require explanation, definition or a statement about their scope or parameters, it may be better to put each aim, question or hypothesis on a separate slide and provide term and construct explanations on the same slide.

The Rationale and Importance of the Focus of the Presentation

This will certainly take more than one slide as some of the key theoretical and empirical literature will be provided as justification for the various statements that are offered here. This material may be divided into sub-sections. For example, the first slide might provide an overview of the key points on rationale and importance while subsequent slides might cover the relevant theoretical and empirical justifications.

An Outline of the Alignment between Gaps in Knowledge and How They Were Investigated

For clarity, a table that places, in column one, the research questions/hypotheses and, in column two, the data sources that were used for each research question/ hypothesis can reveal to the audience both a summary of the key questions/ hypotheses identified in earlier slides and an outline of the type of data that were drawn upon for answering the questions or testing the hypotheses.

Key Aspects of the Methodology

Key information may include research approach, design, data sources, data collection, data analysis, reliability and validity. Each of these areas may be outlined on a separate slide or two of these areas may be outlined on a single slide. It depends on how many points the area needs to refer to.

The Key Findings in Relation to the Stated Research Questions/Hypotheses

The most important findings, in relation to the title of the presentation and the research questions/hypotheses, should be presented.

A Discussion of the Contribution of the Research to the Field

This may include a discussion about (a) why the findings occurred as they did, with reference to theory and earlier research and (b) what they offer the field of knowledge (e.g. what they add to existing theoretical explanations and predictions, to our understanding of effective methodological approaches and to the world of practice).

An Outline of Any Limitations and Recommendations for Further Research to Develop Knowledge within the Field

In Box 7.5, the twenty slides, covering the areas of content referred to above, illustrate how a presentation might be structured.

BOX 7.5   AN EXAMPLE OF THE FOCUS OF TWENTY POWERPOINT SLIDES

Slide number	Slide focus
1	Title of presentation
2	Overview of presentation
3	Aims/research questions/hypotheses and key definitions
4	Aims/research questions/hypotheses and key definitions
5	Overview of rationale and importance
6	Literature justification
7	Literature justification
8	Literature justification
9	Gaps and data sources
10	Key aspects of methodology
11	Key aspects of methodology
12	Key aspects of methodology
13	Findings
14	Findings
15	Findings
16	Discussion of contribution
17	Discussion of contribution
18	Discussion of contribution
19	Limitations
20	Further research

---

108 Advice/Feedback on the Writing of Other Texts

An example of a 20-minute power-point presentation is provided in Appendix C. Amongst other features of note, it will be seen that (1) the slides are uncluttered as a result of minimal content, (2) the slides are attractively designed and frequently include visual components to clarify meaning and (3) there are not too many slides on any one aspect of the presentation (e.g. only key features of the literature background are presented).

A Mock Presentation

Once the slides have been prepared, students should test the time it takes to present them. A mock presentation in front of other students and supervisors will enable feedback to be provided about the clarity and comprehensibility of the presentation. Supervisors should explain to students that each time they prepare for and deliver a PowerPoint presentation they will learn new things about themselves as presenters, about what works well, about what needs to be different next time and about what audiences find effective.

Submitting a Written Version of the Presentation for Publication

Conference presentations are sometimes published in an anthology of papers or in a book of proceedings. On other occasions, students may use the conference presentation and feedback they receive from members of the audience to shape the work for publication as a journal article. Irrespective of which type of publication students choose, advice about how to meet the specific requirements and expectations of editors should be offered by supervisors. In the next section of this chapter, I explain what students need to know when preparing a manuscript for publication.

PART THREE: WRITING A JOURNAL ARTICLE

Writing a journal article from part of a dissertation can be quite a daunting task for many students, especially if they want to do this during the dissertation journey and if they try to do it without advice from their supervisor. The aim of this section, then, is to outline the advice I think students can benefit from before they start writing. The advice I offer covers the following areas: (a) understanding the key stages associated with turning an area of their research into a journal article; (b) understanding the typical expectations of editors and the criteria they use to evaluate a manuscript's suitability for publication; and (c) typical areas of weakness in the writing of an article that can be overcome with good pre-writing advice and post-writing feedback on an initial draft.

The Key Stages Associated with Turning Research into a Journal Article

Essentially, there are ten key stages in preparing for and writing an article for publication.

Selecting the Focus of the Article

This involves the selection of a section of the dissertation that will offer something new to a journal's readership. It is wise to choose only one of the main questions or hypotheses of the dissertation because anything more than this is likely to limit the depth of reporting and discussion. Many students are lucky enough to be able to co-author with one or more of their supervisors. If this is the case, it is a good idea to select an important issue or question but not the most important or significant one for the field because this is the area that students should be allowed to author by themselves after they have been through an article-writing apprenticeship with their supervisor(s). Before starting a co-authored article, an agreement should be reached about the line-up of authors and their relative workloads.

Selecting an Appropriate Journal

Having decided on which part of the dissertation will be reported in the article, the second stage is to select a journal that is likely to be interested in the research. There are five factors that can be considered when making this selection. First, the website of the journal will typically outline its areas of interest and indicate who the readership is likely to be. If there is an alignment between the area you have selected from the dissertation and one or more of the journal's areas of interest, the next factor to consider may be the number of issues the journal publishes each year. This may be an important factor if you want to have your work published sooner rather than later. The third factor for consideration might be its international reputation. Some journals can be classified as international whereas others are more typically seen as regional or local. The fourth factor might be the journal's ranking and its impact factor. I would generally advise students to aim first for a journal with a high or a growing impact factor but if such a journal rejects the manuscript, a journal with a lower impact factor can then be considered. Finally, it is helpful to look at other articles that have been published recently in the journal as this will provide insights into the standard of work that gets published in the journal.

Stages in Drafting the Manuscript

Once the first two decisions have been made, attention can then focus on drafting the initial version of the manuscript. This can be achieved by means of the ten steps presented in Box 7.6.

110 Advice/Feedback on the Writing of Other Texts

BOX 7.6 STAGES IN DRAFTING A MANUSCRIPT

(a) Write an initial abstract for the manuscript so there is clarity about (i) the focus of the manuscript, (ii) the relevant findings that will be reported, (iii) the relevant aspects of the methodology and (iv) the relevant literature background and discussion/conclusion points. You will note here that decisions are made first about the research that is to be reported and then about the literature, discussion and conclusions as they need to relate directly to the findings and associated methodology.

(b) Write up the results or findings that are relevant to the research question/hypothesis

(c) Outline aspects of the methodology that informed the findings

(d) Present the background theoretical, empirical and non-research literature that is relevant to the research question/hypothesis focus

(e) Discuss the findings in light of the selected literature

(f) Draw conclusions on the basis of the findings and discussion that has been presented

(g) Write an introduction to the article

(h) Decide on the title of the article

(i) Revise the abstract in light of the full draft

(j) Prepare the final draft once headings, tables, figures, references and appendices have been checked against the journal's guidelines and recently published articles in the journal

---

Review by a Colleague and Revision Where Recommended

Most supervisors are willing to read their students' manuscripts and offer advice on how they might be improved. This will happen automatically, of course, if the supervisor is a co-author of the manuscript. Sometimes, students may seek comments from their peers on a quid pro quo basis. Some of the comments that are offered may not necessarily be ones that the authors want to act upon but at least students should be encouraged to carefully consider all advice before revising a manuscript.

Submit the Manuscript to the Journal

Manuscripts are typically submitted online nowadays so a careful read of what needs to be submitted, in addition to the manuscript itself, should precede the online submission. Parts of the manuscript may need to be submitted as separate files so it is important to find out what is required before starting the submission process. Journal websites always contain specific guidelines about the submission process and these need to be read carefully and adhered to equally carefully. An example of a typical set of submission guidelines can be found in Appendix D of this book.

Consider the Editor's and Reviewers' Response to Your Manuscript

Once the manuscript has been received, the editor(s) will read the manuscript and make a decision about whether or not to send it out for external review. If they consider the manuscript is not suitable for their journal, they will usually let you know quite quickly. If they think it has potential, they will send it out for double blind peer review. Generally speaking, this process can take anything up to three months.

Decide How to Respond to the Editor's/Reviewers' Comments

Once authors have received the editor's response (if the manuscript has not been sent out for external review) or the editor's response together with that of the reviewers (i.e. if the manuscript has been sent out for external review), they are in a position to decide what to do next. This, of course, will depend on which of the three types of response the editors and reviewers decide on: reject; revise and resubmit; accept as is. The third option is rarely offered. If the manuscript is rejected, the reviewers' comments should be considered carefully before a revision is made and the manuscript is sent to a new journal. If the response is to revise and resubmit, the comments and advice of the editor need to be noted carefully. The comments from the reviewers also need to be considered carefully but it is not essential that all of the suggestions or recommendations be adopted if a case can be made for not adopting them. Once these comments have been considered, the manuscript should be revised and returned to the editor, together with a covering letter that explains which recommendations have been adopted, where these can be found in the manuscript and which recommendations have not been adopted and why. Where requirements are stated, authors need to follow them.

The Editor's Response to your Revision

Having read the revision, the editor (and often after consultation with one or more of the reviewers) will make a decision about whether the manuscript is suitable for publication. Sometimes, further minor amendments will be asked for but, typically, the editor will let you know if the journal is going to publish the work.

112 Advice/Feedback on the Writing of Other Texts

Proofread the Publisher's Proofs

Once the final version of the manuscript has been accepted, the journal's type-setters will format the manuscript for publication. Before publication, however, you will be required to check the proofs to make sure everything has been correctly presented. This is not an opportunity to make any further revisions.

Await Publication

Speed of publication varies from journal to journal. Editors will usually be able to signal an intended publication issue/month.

Understanding the Criteria that Editors Use to Evaluate the Manuscript's Suitability for Publication

Many journals outline on their websites the criteria they use when making a decision about whether or not to publish a manuscript. Some of the key questions they ask themselves are provided in Box 7.7.

BOX 7.7 CRITERIA FOR THE ACCEPTANCE OF A MANUSCRIPT

1 Does the manuscript address an important problem or issue in the field of knowledge?
2 Does the manuscript represent a significant advancement in knowledge?
3 Is the manuscript likely to be of interest to the journal's readership?
4 Is the manuscript sufficiently focused as a journal article?
5 Is the manuscript grounded in appropriate theory?
6 Is the relevant existing literature acknowledged?
7 For manuscripts that discuss issues in essay form:

   (a) Is the author's presentation clear, sound and logical?
   (b) Are the author's claims well supported?
   (c) Are the author's conclusions reasonable?

8 For manuscripts that report on empirical research:

   (a) Are the context, subjects, data collection and data analysis adequately described?
   (b) Is the study valid, reliable and replicable?
   (c) Are the results presented in a fair and balanced manner?
   (d) Are the conclusions supported by the study's findings?

Advice/Feedback on the Writing of Other Texts **113**

9 Is the manuscript well written?

(a) Are the functional requirements (introduction, literature review, methodology, etc.) of an article presented?

(b) Is the manuscript clearly and rhetorically structured?

(c) Does the manuscript meet the stated expectations of the journal with regard to formatting and word length?

Typical Areas of Weakness in the Writing of a Journal Article

In spite of the advice that students may be given on how to write an effective journal article, there are a number of areas of weakness that reviewers and editors often identify in their feedback comments. Appendix E identifies some of the typical comments that editors give authors about why they are not going to send the manuscript out for review. These comments refer to more global concerns about the appropriateness of the subject matter of the manuscript and major flaws or weaknesses in the rationale and methodological design of the research. In the remainder of this chapter, some of the key weaknesses of specific parts or sections of the manuscript are identified.

Introduction

Lack of Clarity around the Focus of the Manuscript

This is sometimes an issue because the introduction fails to clearly identify the research questions/hypotheses that frame the focus of the manuscript. Sometimes, in addition to a presentation of research questions/hypotheses, other areas of interest are also mentioned in the introduction and, as a result, the reader may be confused about the intended focus of the article.

The Context of the Area of Focus May Be Too Vague or Not Be Presented

Some research questions/hypotheses could be situated in more than one discipline so some degree of clarity about the context is helpful in the introduction.

Insufficient Explanation about Why the Area of Focus Is Important or Significant

Most student authors understand that the importance and significance of the area of focus should be referred to but often the explanation focuses on only one factor. For example, most students realise the importance of stating

114 Advice/Feedback on the Writing of Other Texts

what the research and its findings contribute to the field but often there is no consideration about who it is important for and about its potential contribution to theory-building.

Key Constructs and Terms May Not Be Clearly Defined

On first mention, it is important that key constructs and terms are explained. Two considerations are important in this regard: (a) the definition or glossing of a construct or term should not be more than an overarching definition in the introduction and (b) it should be one that reveals exactly how it is used in the research that is being reported. Sometimes, student authors will quote other authors but, in doing so, can fail to define the construct or term as it has been used in the research. Another issue can be the inclusion of too much information for an introduction.

The Absence of a Clear Line of Argument for the Focus of the Manuscript

Readers need to know what the central argument of the manuscript will be. Sometimes, student authors will only give a partial explanation of the focus of their argument or fail to explicitly establish the relationship between what is said and the actual focus of the manuscript (as indicated by the research questions/hypotheses).

A deconstruction and discussion of model examples of effective article introductions is one of the best ways of addressing these shortcomings.

Literature Review

Irrelevant Literature

It is quite common for some of the literature that is presented in the literature review component of the manuscript to be irrelevant to the central focus of the research being reported.

The Literature May Not Be Related Directly to the Focus of the Manuscript

This is a very common problem if student authors fail to use the literature to background and justify the research focus of their manuscript. Presenting the literature as it might be found in a textbook or academic reader (even if it is relevant) is unlikely to tell the reader how it is relevant to the research focus.

The Theoretical Component of the Literature Review May Be Insufficiently Stated

If the student's research focus has been informed more by empirical gaps than by theoretical questions, it is quite common for student authors to only give a cursory reference to the theoretical thinking behind the research. A lack of explanation about why the area of focus is an issue or problem or about what theoretical perspectives can explain or predict, and why, are areas that are sometimes given in the feedback of reviewers and editors.

The Review May Not Be Up-To-Date

If student authors are writing their first manuscript some considerable time after they last revised the literature review chapter of their dissertation, it may be that more recent publications need to be included in the manuscript. Reviewers, as experts in the field, are likely to be well aware of these so student authors need to update their literature search before finalising this section of their manuscript.

An Advance Organiser that Outlines the Argument of the Review May Not Have Been Provided

The inclusion of such a paragraph at the beginning of the review can give the reader a good overview of what the argument will be in the review. If this is provided, student writers are likely to be more focused and logical in the development of the argument and how it leads to an announcement about the focus of the research that is to be reported.

Methodology

Insufficient Clear Detail about How the Research Was Conducted

Gaps in the methodological components that are relevant to the research that is reported in the manuscript are common. Given that much of what has been included in the methodology chapter of the dissertation needs to also be presented in the manuscript, it is understandable that student authors can struggle with down-sizing the detail and may leave out steps or information that readers would need to know if they were to replicate the study. Perhaps the most problematic area of the methodology section of the manuscript is reporting about how the data were analysed.

Unnecessary Detail

On the other hand, student authors can sometimes include information that they should be able to assume readers of the journal will know. For instance,

116 Advice/Feedback on the Writing of Other Texts

there is no need to provide a detailed description of statistical tests that may have been used because readers will most likely know what, for example, an ANOVA is and why it is used. If they don't know this, they will at least know how to find out.

An Incoherent Outline of Processes and Procedures

There can be a tendency for some student authors to do a cut and paste from their dissertation, meaning that the coherence between one piece of information and the next may suffer. Student authors often need feedback on the importance of creating a line of argument in this section rather than just seeing it as a 'shopping list' of facts.

Results or Findings

In a journal article, the findings and discussion are sometimes presented as one section rather than as two sections. Doing so can enable the author to economise on space and make the discussion more immediate to the findings. For the sake of clarity here, I refer to them as two sections.

Not All Findings May Need To Be Presented

Readers are more likely to be interested in the key findings of a research question so findings that emerged in the research for subsidiary questions or as a result of a post hoc analysis may not be of sufficient interest to readers. On the other hand, it does need to be mentioned that some minor details may be relevant if the manuscript has focused on a subsidiary question rather than on one of the main questions.

Findings May Not Always Be Directly Related to the Focus of the Manuscript

This issue is more about being explicit in relating the findings to the research questions/hypotheses. Sometimes, student authors will leave it for the reader to make the connection between what the finding is showing and what the question/hypothesis stated.

The Findings May Not Always Observe Publication Conventions

This can be an issue if tables and figures or in-text references and the list of references do not conform to the journal's conventions (e.g. the latest APA conventions).

The Findings Are Not Always Explained for the Non-expert Reader

This is more likely to be an issue if the student's research involved technical analysis (e.g. statistical testing). While it is expected that the findings will be explained in technical terms, it is also expected that each finding will be explained in non-technical language for the non-expert reader and be directly related to what it found about the research question/hypothesis.

Discussion of Findings

Insufficient Discussion of Findings in Relation to Theory and Other Related Research

Student authors are generally well focused on identifying the extent to which their findings support/corroborate those of other research or when their findings may be different to those of other research but they tend to be weak when it comes to explaining why similarities and differences may have occurred. In this regard, there may be a missed opportunity to consider (a) what and how their theoretical perspectives can explain the results or (b) similarities and differences in the methodologies of the studies being referred to (for example, the fact that different variables across studies may have had an impact on different outcomes).

Insufficient Explanation of Findings in Relation to the Wider Picture

It takes a degree of reflection to be able to see the relationship between one's own findings and everything that has been outlined in the literature review (theory, research and practice). A failure to do so can mean a lack of claims and conclusions about how the field may move forward. Some students are reluctant to step outside the confines of their own research or feel that they do not have the authority to do this.

Claims, Recommendations and Conclusions Need to Be Justified from the Findings

Some students are rather too quick to offer all sorts of claims and conclusions that have not arisen from their research findings. On the other hand, some students have the evidence in their research findings but fail to draw on them to explain to the reader the grounds upon which they are making certain claims.

Conclusions

A Statement about the Overall Contribution of the Research to the Field May Be Omitted

The conclusion section of a manuscript can vary considerably from discipline to discipline. In some disciplines, it may be little more than a wrap of what has been more extensively discussed in the discussion of results section. In other disciplines, it may be expected that the conclusion will focus on an overarching statement about the contribution of the research to the field. Whether or not this focus is presented in the discussion or in the conclusion is not as important as the need for it to be presented somewhere.

A Failure to Think about What the Author Wants the Reader to Take from a Reading of the Manuscript

A final remarks section or the final few sentences of the manuscript should strongly reinforce what the manuscript has been about and leave the reader with a positive feeling about what it offers the field and what may be developed as a result of the findings and conclusions that have been presented. Ending on a positive forward-looking note should be the aim of any writer. Too often, manuscripts just peter out.

APPENDIX A

Some Key Aspects of the Published Research Informing the Focus of this Book

The aim of this appendix is to provide readers who are interested in some of the research informing the advice and feedback recommended in this book with an overview of some of the published literature (1) on issues or difficulties that second language (L2) students may encounter as undergraduates or as graduate students when drafting chapters of their dissertations, (2) on what supervisors say they often provide written feedback on when assessing their students' early drafts of chapters, (3) on the feedback that some supervisors actually provide their students with when giving written feedback on-text comments and (4) what students say they value about the written feedback they receive.

General writing issues experienced by second language (L2) student writers of English at both undergraduate and postgraduate levels have been the subject of on-going research for a number of decades. While much attention has been given to identifying difficulties at the sentence and paragraph levels (e.g. Casanave & Hubbard, 1992; Cooley & Lewkowicz, 1997; Dong, 1998), less attention has been given to investigations of the extent to which these and other difficulties continue to be issues for postgraduate L2 students writing their first thesis or their doctoral dissertation in English.

Several studies have investigated supervisor perceptions of the difficulties that postgraduate L2 students may encounter. Casanave and Hubbard's (1992) survey of 82 supervisors across 28 departments at Stanford University reported that L2 doctoral students often have more difficulties than first language (L1) writers of English. The issues that they identified were more prevalent at the sentence level (grammatical accuracy and appropriateness, vocabulary appropriateness, spelling and punctuation accuracy) than at the paragraph level. Similar findings were reported by Cooley and Lewkowicz (1997) in their study of 105 supervisors across nine faculties at the University of Hong Kong. The supervisors in

120 Appendix A

this study explained that while difficulties with surface forms and structures (e.g. the accurate use of the English article system and subject-verb agreement) can be irritating, they are less problematic than difficulties affecting the development of coherent ideas and arguments. In her study of two universities in the USA, Dong (1998) reported that L2 postgraduate students experience difficulty with the sequencing and development of propositions and with the use of transitions between propositions and topics. The particular effect of these difficulties on overall communicative success was commented on by James (1984) in his case study of a Brazilian doctoral student at the University of Manchester. He categorised the effects according to whether they resulted in a breakdown of meaning, a blurring of meaning or a distraction that had little effect on overall meaning. Each of the authors of these studies conclude that while L2 students may have more difficulty overcoming sentence level difficulties than L1 students, this difference is less evident in the discourse at the paragraph level. L1 students can find argument construction as much of a challenge as L2 student writers. Additionally, both L1 and L2 student writers can encounter issues with understanding what characterises the dissertation as a genre (and the part-genres or chapters of the dissertation) and with understanding the discipline-specific expectations and conventions of their supervisors.

Issues with understanding the generic and discipline-specific characteristics of the dissertation as an academic research genre (including its part-genres) have been identified to some extent by studies that have investigated supervisor perceptions of dissertation-writing difficulties (Allison, Cooley, Lewkowicz & Nunan, 1998; Basturkmen & Bitchener, 2005; Bitchener & Basturkmen, 2006; Casanave & Hubbard, 1992; Casanave & Li, 2008; Dong, 1998; Jenkins, Jordan & Weiland, 1993; Paltridge & Starfield, 2007). This body of research reports that dissertation students are often uncertain about how the content might be most effectively organised. While the structuring and positioning of an argument in relation to the wider literature can be challenging for both L1 and L2 students, the prevailing opinion of supervisors is that L2 students are likely to have more difficulty than L1 students when critiquing the published research, when reaching a resolution when differing theoretical perspectives need to be assessed in terms of their relevance and appropriateness and when weighing up the significance of their own research findings (Cadman, 1997; Dong, 1998; Frost, 1999; O'Connell & Jin, 2001). Additionally, it is noted that students who have studies in an epistemological context, where the creation of argument and counterargument and critical evaluation of published work may be less encouraged, are more likely to encounter these issues. From these insights, it is clear that dissertation-writing students need to understand and develop both generic and discipline-specific knowledge and skills if they are to be successfully enculturated into the academic community they are working within.

To meet these needs, some form of explicit instruction needs to be available to students. If the dissertation research is one component of the doctoral qualification, alongside other components such as course-work papers or courses, students will likely receive instruction on what is expected in carrying out doctoral-level research and in writing up a doctoral dissertation. Other doctoral students may not start their doctoral journey with this knowledge. In such circumstances, supervisory feedback has an even greater importance. As several researcher/supervisors have noted, feedback is therefore central to the supervisory process as it constitutes a major, if not the major, form of instruction some students are likely to receive (Benesch, 2000; Hyland & Tse, 2004; Kumar & Stracke, 2007).

So what are the key purposes or functions of feedback? According to Hyland (2009), feedback helps students understand the norms and values of different disciplines and, as a result, enables students to be enculturated into the disciplinary literacies and practices of the discipline. Adding to this overall aim, Sofoulis (1997) suggests that feedback is designed to help students discover their individual stance in relation to those of others in the field, to help students gain recognition for the research they are reporting on and to help them develop their own voice in relation to the contribution their own work offers the discipline. Essentially, then, feedback is designed to help students become independent researchers and writers. At the most practical level, feedback can be seen as an assessment of what has been done/written and as advice on what should be considered next to help the student move forward towards achieving the standard of performance expected of a doctoral graduate.

Given the difficulties that doctoral students may encounter and given the purposes of feedback, it is then important to understand the nature of and the focus of the feedback that supervisors say they give their doctoral students. One study by Bitchener, Basturkmen and East (2010) piloted an approach to investigating what supervisors from three discipline areas (Humanities, Sciences/Mathematics, Commerce) say they give their students feedback on. Data from questionnaire and interview responses, together with examples of feedback from samples discussed in the interviews, elicited whether feedback was given on (1) the accuracy, completeness and relevance of the content included in the chapter drafts, (2) what was required and expected for each of the part-genres or chapters, (3) the rhetorical structure and organisation of the discourse, (4) the coherence and cohesion of the arguments presented and (5) the linguistic accuracy and appropriateness of the texts.

Most feedback on content concerned the gaps in subject knowledge content presented in the text. This was especially so with regard to theoretical understanding and coverage. Supervisors from the three disciplines mentioned this issue and added that it was just as much an issue for L1 students as it was for L2 students. However, they tended to be of one voice in suggesting that there was a greater need for feedback to be given to L2 students on the importance of discussing the published literature and their own findings in light of the big picture (introduced in the literature review) and of taking a critical look at what

122 Appendix A

is published. Argument construction was identified by the supervisors in each of the three disciplines as an area in which both L1 and L2 students often needed feedback. Presenting sufficient argument, explanation or justification and then presenting it in a coherent and cohesive manner were identified as key areas for supervisor attention.

With regard to understanding what is typically expected as appropriate content in each of the different part-genres of a traditional dissertation, some supervisors said that they usually did not need to give much feedback on what is expected if the purpose and functions of each part-genre had been discussed before students started writing. More often than not, they said that feedback tended to be provided on how the content was used to support and structure the direction of the argument. This was not seen as an issue for only L2 students.

Feedback on linguistic accuracy was seen as more of an L2 issue and textual examples of feedback discussed in the interviews revealed that more feedback was given on accuracy and appropriateness than on any other area. It was particularly interesting to note that several supervisors did not consider textual markings about accuracy to be feedback. They saw it more as editorial marking and said that they did not want the attention of their students to be drawn away from the more macro issues that needed to be commented on.

From this brief overview of some of the key findings from this exploratory study, it can be seen that the difficulties or issues identified in earlier years in the published literature as those that L2 students may tend to struggle with are indeed those that supervisors say they often need to provide feedback on. The extent to which supervisors provide these different types of feedback to their doctoral students is not something that this study focused on. The aim of the study was to elicit, by means of supervisor self-report data, the range of areas on which they said that they found it was necessary to provide feedback. The researchers suggested that further research be conducted to quantify the response categories so that an understanding of the extent to which they are areas that most supervisors say they comment on can be understood. In this regard, they added that the findings of this study might be used to develop a closed-ended questionnaire that includes a series of behavioural and attitudinal statements requiring Likert-scale responses and ranking.

Taking this study of feedback practices to a more global level, Bitchener (2015) reported on the findings of a study into the kind of feedback that 60 Applied Linguistics supervisors from four universities in the USA (15 participants), two universities in the UK (8 participants), four universities in Australia (21 participants) and six universities in New Zealand (16 participants) typically provide on the different chapters of a traditional dissertation. The first question asked which chapters the supervisors said they needed to provide most content feedback on. In rank order, they said that the greatest amount of feedback was provided on the literature review chapter and, in order, this was followed by the discussion of findings chapter, the introduction chapter, the methodology chapter, the findings or results chapter, the conclusion chapter and the abstract. Arguably, more important were the feedback areas identified for each of these chapters in response to the second research question about what the areas of feedback focus typically are for each chapter and why this is the case. The key areas and reasons are summarised below.

The Introduction Chapter

1   Difficulty addressing the rationale and significance of the study, situating themselves in the study and establishing their voice
2   Need help to explain why the research is needed (apart from filling a gap in the literature)
3   Difficulty identifying the problem
4   Research questions usually need refinement
5   Depends when early draft is written
6   The introduction is crucial and needs to be revised often
7   Scope may need narrowing; 'no need to go back to Aristotle'
8   Need help with how to enter scholarly debates

The Literature Review Chapter(s)

1   Difficult because it serves several purposes
2   Relevance and focus of the literature presented; choices around selectivity are crucial
3   Insufficient explicit argument on purpose of thesis; framing the argument around the research questions; signposting
4   Need to understand and show reader how theoretical and empirical literature relates to the study's focus; understand the relative importance of concepts/issues
5   Missing content needs to be identified

The Methodology Chapter(s)

1   Rationale of methodology is sometimes weak
2   Limited consideration given to methodological approach
3   Replication – could the study be replicated? Descriptive detail sometimes missing
4   Data analysis detail often missing
5   Relationships between current method and other methods used for similar project often not considered
6   Qualitative methodologies often require more advice and feedback than quantitative methodologies

124 Appendix A

The Findings or Results Chapter

1 Structuring and sequencing in relation to research questions (RQs) often an area of weakness
2 Need to focus on key discoveries
3 Statistical analyses often need more explanation
4 Appropriate and adequate data to support claims are often weak
5 Qualitative studies – need to make an argument from examples rather than just using data to exemplify points; relevance of examples can be an issue

The Discussion of Results Chapter

1 Not always consistently and closely based on results; claims and conclusions need to arise specifically from findings
2 Links to literature (theoretical and methodological) not always provided; relationship of findings to methodological approaches and theoretical concepts often weak
3 Discussion can be on two levels: in relation to precise details and to overall focus of RQs
4 Often the question of 'so what?' is not taken as far as it could be

The Conclusion Chapter

1 Explain the big picture/significance of findings for the field
2 Often a need to move conclusions beyond a summary to focus on the study's significance
3 Conclusions often not linked to focus of RQs
4 Include some speculation; consider the way forward

The Abstract

1 Balance across discourse moves given that it is a compressed form while trying to encapsulate the whole thing
2 Balance between being creative and generic
3 Editing is often required
4 Explain the significance of the project

Each of the feedback areas identified in the summaries above are discussed in detail in the various chapters of this book. The findings of the 'global supervision' study, together with my own experience (including both trial and error), have informed the content in the chapters of this book.

So far in this overview of key research informing the focus of this book we have considered (1) some of the early studies that investigated difficulties L2

Appendix A **125**

writers may encounter and (2), in more recent research, what supervisors have said they often need to provide feedback on when assessing the early drafts of the dissertation chapters. In conducting research on the latter, the researchers Bitchener, Basturkmen and East also examined the written feedback that supervisors in New Zealand, across three broad discipline areas (Humanities, Sciences/Mathematics and Commerce), provided as on-text or in-text comments on early drafts of their students' chapters. The findings of this research have been published in Basturkmen, East and Bitchener (2014). From the analysis, the study produced two descriptive frameworks: (1) aspects of the writing commented on and (2) the manner in which the comments are formulated linguistically. It was recognised that comments of this type represent only one type of written feedback and that supervisors typically provide summary comments at the end of the student's text. Whereas the on-script comments may be seen as less planned, considered or processed than the summary comments, they are often all that some students receive.

From an analysis of the comments a four-part classification system was created: (1) content (information, arguments and claims); (2) requirements (expectations for the section and academic conventions, such as APA formatting); (3) cohesion and coherence; and (4) linguistic accuracy and appropriateness. For details and examples of each category, see Basturkmen, East and Bitchener (2014). The analysis of comments also revealed how the supervisors formulated their feedback comments. Drawing on Kumar and Stracke (2007), the descriptive framework created from these comments referred to pragmatic function in order to identify what seemed to be the pragmatic or communicative intention of the comments (e.g. seeking further information; making a recommendation). Three classification categories were created from these comments: (1) those with a referential function (e.g. providing information or corrections); (2) those with a directive function (e.g. eliciting – asking for information or clarification, suggesting or telling the student what to do or not do); and (3) those with an expressive function (e.g. registering a positive or negative response). Examples of these categories can also be found in Basturkmen, East and Bitchener (2014).

So, what did the study find? The first group of findings below concern the four areas on which supervisors gave written feedback or comment. The second group of findings concern the manner in which the feedback comments were formulated.

Group One Findings

1   Most submissions contained written feedback comments on content, linguistic accuracy and requirements.
2   Approximately half the submissions contained comments on cohesion and coherence.

126 Appendix A

3 In Commerce and Science/Mathematics, most contained in order of frequency comments on linguistic accuracy, content and requirements and only a few on cohesion and coherence.
4 In Humanities, content and linguistic accuracy comments were more frequent than those on requirements and very few on cohesion and coherence.
5 It is to be noted that generalisations cannot be concluded given the range of chapter types that were submitted by the supervisors.

Group Two Findings

1 Comments on content and cohesion/coherence were most often directives (e.g. eliciting, suggesting or telling the student what to do). These comments were often quite pragmatically complex insofar as they contained a number of pragmatic acts or functions.
2 Comments on linguistic accuracy/appropriateness were mostly referential (e.g. informing or correcting).
3 Expressive comments were typically found in content feedback.
4 Correction was often communicated by means of reformulations of the students' texts.

A number of reasons have been suggested for these particular patterns and these can be referred to in Basturkmen, East and Bitchener (2014) if readers are interested in these explanations. In reflecting upon these findings for pedagogical practice, caution needs to be exercised given a couple of limitations of scope of the study. The study investigated a small portion of sample texts as many supervisors were not comfortable with analyses being done on their comments and were reluctant to seek their students' permission for research purposes. For this reason, the findings reported above need to be seen as potentially indicative. Second, if further research were to investigate feedback patterns and behaviours, a body of texts from the same part-genre or chapter should be analysed to avoid functional differences between part-genres having an effect on the findings. Comparisons across part-genres as well as within and across disciplines would likely produce more conclusive results for pedagogy. Nevertheless, the findings reported here in this exploratory study are thought-provoking and reveal the need for further investigations into on-text feedback comments.

Thus far in this overview of research findings, attention has been given to what supervisors say they provide feedback on and what analyses of their actual written feedback practices reveal. This, of course, is only part of the story that needs to be told. The other important part is what the students have to say about the feedback they receive from their supervisors. One exploratory study in New Zealand (East, Bitchener & Basturkmen, 2012) investigated the student perspective. In this study, both L1 and L2 student perspectives were sought so it is useful in this appendix to consider any significant differences between the two cohorts of students. From 53 student questionnaire responses and 22 follow-up student interview responses, the study investigated four research questions:

1 What types of written feedback do students report that they receive?
2 What types of written feedback do students report finding the most helpful?
3 What differences, if any, exist between students with English as L1 and English as L2?
4 Based on their experiences with feedback, what recommendations would students make to new supervisors?

Questionnaire responses provided the data (frequencies of particular practices) for research question 1. Interview responses provided the data for an understanding of what the students considered to be effective practices. Two out of every three interview participants had English as an L2. Data were used to answer research questions 2 and 3. For research question 4, the questionnaires and the interviews provided students with the opportunity to make recommendations about the type of feedback practices that they thought new supervisors could benefit from.

So, what did the study find?

For research question 1 about the feedback students said they typically received, the following findings emerged:

1 On the content or subject matter of their work, students said they received more feedback on the relevance of the literature they included in their work and that this was closely followed by requests to rethink how the work was being presented, advice on how to find the literature relevant to their focus and comments on the appropriateness of their methodology.
2 On the organisation and structure of their content, half of the students said they received both specific and overview feedback on the effectiveness of the organisation of their chapter drafts while a smaller percentage said they received feedback on where they could edit or condense irrelevant material.
3 On the accuracy of their language, nearly half of the students said that received feedback on their choice of vocabulary, the appropriateness of their register and an identification of where there were issues with their grammar, spelling and punctuation.

For research question 2 on the types of feedback the students said they found most helpful, some differences between L1 and L2 students emerged. For L1 students, the following issues were important:

1 They wishes to receive direct feedback, meaning specific feedback, with the overall organisation of their writing.
2 They preferred less direct comments that challenged their thinking and prompted them to find their own answers.

128 Appendix A

3   Although they said that they appreciated direct feedback on language, they added that it was seen as secondary to feedback that challenged them intellectually.
4   They said they valued the opportunity to discuss the feedback.

L2 students referred to the following issues as those they valued:

1   They said that they appreciated direct or specific feedback on language.
2   They said that they valued balanced feedback that included direct feedback on both language and organisation as well as more indirect prompting.
3   They said that they were not always sure about how to interpret the feedback they received and that more direct feedback might help.
4   They said they valued feedback that promoted autonomy and that helped them develop their intellectual capability.

For research question 3 on differences between L1 and L2 preferences, very few differences were discovered. While L2 students tended to value direct feedback a little more than L1 students especially on feedback they were not sure about how to interpret and on the accuracy of their writing in English, both cohorts valued approaches that encouraged them to (1) become more independent of their supervisors over time and (2) develop their intellectual capabilities. A dialogic relationship between supervisor and student was seen as important by both L1 and L2 students.

For research question 4 on advice that the students considered important for new supervisors, they following recommendations were offered:

1   Give both written and oral feedback with a view to feed forward;
2   Make positive and constructive comments alongside critique;
3   Understand the project;
4   Give suggestions but do not be too directive.

For a detailed analysis and discussion of the findings of this study, see East, Basturkmen and Bitchener (2012).

Given the exploratory nature of this study, the following recommendations can be offered for further research into the student perspective on written feedback:

1   Compare the responses of students from different cultural and pedagogical backgrounds.
2   Collect data from (1) a more closed-ended questionnaire that includes a series of behavioural and attitudinal statements and (2) Likert-scale and ranking questions.
3   Compare the type of feedback given at early and later stages of the supervisory process Longitudinal research would help to identify any differences in feedback practices.

The aim of this overview of research on (1) earlier publications about students' writing difficulties at the graduate/postgraduate level and (2) more recent research on both the supervisor and student perspectives on written feedback, was to identify from empirical research what supervisors and students say they provide/receive feedback on, so that readers, with an interest in what motivated the pedagogical content focus of this book, could receive a snapshot of this body of work before (1) referring to the specific reports of the research in the books and journal articles referred to in this appendix and (2) reading the chapters of this book.

APPENDIX B

Code of Practice for Supervisors and Student Responsibilities

Source: Auckland University of Technology Postgraduate Handbook 2017, pp. 53–55 and pp. 56–57

General Responsibilities of Supervisors

The principal responsibility of research supervisors (whether primary or secondary) is to be accessible advisors who encourage and assist students to develop standards of achievement which will result in a thesis/dissertation that meets the criteria for successful completion.

Prior to supervising at AUT all supervisors who are new to AUT are required to attend a workshop facilitated by the Graduate Research School (GRS). This seminar introduces supervisors to AUT processes for supervision and administration of research students. Completion of the workshop enables the supervisor to be added to the University supervisor register which is a requirement prior to approval as a supervisor.

Supervisors, in conjunction with the Associate Dean (Postgraduate) will assist students to fulfil all academic and administrative requirements promptly, satisfactorily and to a scholarly level.

Supervisors, in consultation with the student, organise regular contact with students (a minimum of once a month) for formal discussions, constructive evaluation and feedback in relation to satisfactory progress. The type and amount of contact between supervisors and students may vary, depending on the developing experience and expertise of the student, the nature of the study being undertaken and the amount of practical work involved. This and other requirements are best identified in a Research Supervision Agreement which is completed with all the supervisory team.

Administrative and Academic Responsibilities

As part of the academic supervision of a student's progress, supervisors (whether primary or secondary) are:

Appendix B **131**

- Required to be familiar with the University regulations governing postgraduate programmes with regard to all information given to students;
- Responsible for drawing the attention of the student to relevant aspects of the regulations and ensure they report as required to the relevant faculty postgraduate committee and/or the University Postgraduate Board on prescribed matters;
- Required to discuss intellectual property issues with the student and assess the commercial potential of the research;
- Responsible for submitting ethics applications in consultation with the student (see Research Ethics Section of the Postgraduate Handbook);
- Responsible for guiding and challenging the student's development as a researcher, thesis writer and critic.

On appointment, a primary supervisor must be an AUT academic staff member and will have overall responsibility for the administrative welfare of students in such matters as:

- The coordination and guidance involved in academic supervision;
- Notifying the faculty postgraduate committee of recommendations for appointment of additional supervisors or changes to the supervisory team;
- The responsibility for guiding the student through the ethical approval process;
- Monitoring reports on student progress toward completion of research;
- Nominating examiners in consultation with the supervisory team;
- Ensuring students format their work appropriate to the pathways undertaken;
- Signing the lodgement form to accompany the thesis/dissertation for examination, testifying that requirements for the thesis/dissertation meet the standards and requirements for examination. These include appropriate format of the work as stated in the Postgraduate Handbook, signing the attestation statement of own work, checking all appendices and forms (e.g. Ethics) are included and that all work has been completed to the satisfaction of the supervisor/s and declared ready for examination.

As part of the academic supervision of a student's progress supervisors (either primary or secondary) are responsible for:

- Negotiating and agreeing to the student's topic;
- Responsible for drawing to the attention of the student relevant aspects of the regulations and ensure that they report as required to the relevant committee;
- Monitoring progress of students and completing each semester the progress report with the student;
- Meeting/contact with the student a minimum of once every month;
- Advising students about University resources available to them so that they are able to make full and proper use of appropriate data sources and resources to assist their research development;

132 Appendix B

- Assisting students with the development of the research proposal and submission to faculty postgraduate committees for approval and submission to the University Postgraduate Board for doctoral and Master of Philosophy proposals;
- Assisting students in planning an appropriate course of collateral reading, suggesting relevant background reading and giving advice on the literature review;
- Providing guidance on the theoretical frameworks, models, methodology, methods and standards of research;
- Submitting applications to the University's Ethics Committee (AUTEC) or other ethics approval body as appropriate through working with the student and ensuring that the student understands the principles and procedures of the relevant ethics committee, and that research projects are of an acceptable ethical standard. It is important to note that the application is in the name of the supervisor;
- Advising students of the aims, scope and presentation of the thesis/ dissertation, monitoring and discussing progress throughout candidature and commenting critically on the final draft;
- Discussing, assessing and guiding the progress of students at regular intervals;
- Giving guidance on necessary completion dates of successive stages of the work so that the whole may be submitted within the scheduled time;
- Assisting students with recording, planning and reviewing progress between contact/meetings, and indicating goals for the next period;
- Providing feedback on written work with constructive criticism and within a reasonable time;
- Encouraging students to practice dissemination of research results, for example, presenting seminars, submitting articles for publication, presenting work at exhibitions, submitting work for peer and/or public review;
- Advising a student of any inadequacy of progress or of standards of work below that generally expected;
- Documenting progress, issues and concerns regularly.

Student Responsibilities

The responsibilities of students include:

- Selecting and negotiating a topic for thesis/dissertation in consultation with their supervisor(s) and submitting a proposal to the relevant postgraduate committee; refining and negotiating a formal research proposal in consultation with the faculty and submitting a proposal to the faculty postgraduate committee;
- Working with the supervisor to obtain approval from the University Ethics Committee and/or other ethical approval as appropriate;

Appendix B **133**

- Completing a supervision agreement in consultation with the supervisor/s;
- Maintaining contact with the supervisor at least once every month, attending meetings and seminars scheduled by the supervisors, and others that contribute to the completion of the research and production of the thesis/ dissertation;
- Discussing with the supervisor the type of guidance and comment they find most helpful and agreeing on a schedule of meetings;
- Responding to arrangements proposed for supervision and the advice and instruction given by the supervisor;
- Maintaining the progress of research, especially written work, to meet the stages and timeframe agreed with the supervisor, to facilitate feedback before the next stage;
- Taking the initiative in raising problems and difficulties, however elementary they may seem;
- Timely progress reports on their work;
- Providing peer support and feedback to other students as appropriate.

APPENDIX C

Sample 20-Minute PowerPoint Slide Presentation

A COMPARISON OF IRAN'S EFL AND NEW ZEALAND'S ESL TEACHERS' BELIEFS AND CLASSROOM PRACTICES IN PROVIDING INTERACTIONAL FEEDBACK

OUTLINE OF PRESENTATION

- My Story
- Aims of the Study
- Definition of Key Terms
- Research Questions
- Rationale & Significance of the Study
- Theoretical Basis
- Previous Studies
- Methodology
- Timetable for Completion

My Story

AIMS OF THE STUDY

1) To examine the relationship between Iranian EFL and New Zealand ESL teachers' **beliefs** (about the value of interactional feedback in L2 acquisition) and their classroom **practices**,

2) To investigate the **extent** to which there is a match/mismatch between teachers' beliefs and classroom practices on IF

3) If there is any mismatch, determine what **factors** could have contributed to it

*The aim is **not** to identify mismatches and make judgements, but to investigate the **relationship** between teachers' beliefs and practices and inform teachers of the **extent** of the relationship and improve teachers' self-awareness in this regard.*

Definitions of Key Terms:

Interactional Feedback (IF): The feedback that is generated in response to both linguistically erroneous and communicatively inappropriate utterances that learners produce during conversational interaction (Nassaji, 2015).

⟹ Teachers' feedback on learners' oral errors (Mackey 2007)

EFL (English as a Foreign Language): Learning English in a country where it is not the common language

ESL (English as a Second Language): Learning English in an English speaking country

Definitions of Key Terms:

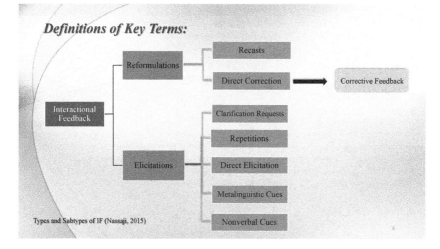

Types and Subtypes of IF (Nassaji, 2015)

RESEARCH QUESTIONS

RQ1. What **beliefs** do (a) Iranian EFL and (b) NZ ESL teachers hold about IF?

RQ2. How do (a) Iranian EFL and (b) NZ ESL teachers **practise** IF?

RQ3. How do Iranian EFL & NZ ESL teachers **compare** with regards to IF beliefs and practices?

RQ4. To what **extent** is there a match/mismatch between teachers' beliefs and classroom practices on IF?

RQ5. What **factors** could have contributed to any mismatch?

RATIONALE OF THE STUDY

1) It is important to investigate what teachers <u>think</u>, <u>know</u> and <u>believe</u>, and the relationship of these mental constructs to what teachers <u>do</u> in the language teaching classrooms (Borg, 2003).

➢ It is generally assumed that teachers' beliefs provide a basis for *action* (Borg, 2011).

⁃ The decisions that teachers make in classrooms can be affected by their *beliefs* (Arnett & Turnbull, 2008).

RATIONALE OF THE STUDY (CONT.)

2) Although literature shows that teachers' use of IF can lead to language development, there are two main issues which are still unclear:

1. What are the beliefs of language teacher about IF?
2. Do their beliefs align with their provision of IF?

⟹ This study intends to fill this **gap** by investigating the beliefs and practices of both ESL and EFL language teachers with regards to IF.

RATIONALE OF THE STUDY (CONT.)

3) This research is also motivated by Borg's (2003, 2015) and Mori's (2011) calls for investigation into teachers' beliefs on *oral feedback.*

• Basturkmen et al. (2004) and Basturkmen (2012) have pointed to the lack of research that investigates a <u>mismatch</u> between teacher beliefs and classroom practices, and the possible <u>factors</u> underlying such mismatches.

⟹ This study intends to take up these scholars' calls for investigation.

RATIONALE OF THE STUDY (CONT.)

4) The focus of this study is unique in that it aims to examine *teachers' side* of the story about IF, an area which has not received much attention in SLA research.

⟹ This study will be first to investigate similarities/differences between the Iranian EFL and New Zealand's ESL contexts from a teacher belief point of view.

SIGNIFICANCE AND CONTRIBUTION

- 1) **Theory** building

- 2) Providing **empirical** knowledge

- 3) Contribution to classroom **pedagogy**

SIGNIFICANCE OF THE STUDY (THEORETICALLY)

Contributes to theories of second language acquisition by focusing on :

1. teachers' beliefs and perception about IF

2. teachers' actual classroom practices regarding IF

3. the relationship between beliefs and practices on IF

SIGNIFICANCE OF THE STUDY (EMPIRICALLY)

1) Adds to the existing research on IF by incorporating only the *teachers' side of the story.*

2) Contributes to researchers' understanding of IF practices, and assist teachers in achieving a more detailed knowledge of what, how, when, why to correct errors.

3) Advances the understanding of both teachers and researchers on teachers' beliefs and assist teachers to detect, alter, or substitute those tacit beliefs with appropriate alternatives (El-Okda, 2005).

SIGNIFICANCE OF THE STUDY (PEDAGOGICALLY)

1) To bring to attention the typical teacher beliefs on IF, and enable teachers to *support* learners more effectively in their efforts for second language development.

2) To emphasize the *central role* of teachers in language classrooms, and encourage *teacher educators* to contribute more to the development of quality amongst teachers.

3) To create awareness about the *relationship* between teachers' beliefs and classroom practices, and help them adjust their feedback practices where necessary.

REVIEW OF LITERATURE (THEORY) (CONT.)

Why IF is considered important for SLA

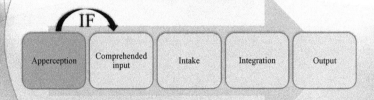

Model of Second Language Acquisition (Gass, 1997)

REVIEW OF LITERATURE (EMPIRICAL STUDIES ON IF) (CONT.)

- **The *effectiveness* of IF in learners' second language development**

(e.g. Ammar & Spada, 2006; Ellis et al., 2006; Kaivanpanah et al., 2015; Kartchava and Ammar, 2014; Mackey et al., 2007; Mackey et al., 2000; Oliver & Mackey, 2003; Russel, 2014; Shabani & Ghasem Dizani, 2015; Yang & Lyster, 2010)

An Important Note

- Many factors can facilitate or impede the *effectiveness* of IF that teachers provide to their learners (e.g. *type of error corrected, learner characteristics, and teacher characteristics*);

- One under-reported factor is **teachers' beliefs** about IF

What is teacher belief?

The *unobservable* aspect of teaching that includes what teachers think, know, and believe (Borg, 2003, 2009).

REVIEW OF LITERATURE (TEACHER BELIEF) (CONT.)

- All teachers hold **beliefs** about learning and teaching which reflect their *personal values, ideologies* (Verloop et al., 2001), and *philosophies* of teaching (Richards, 1996).

- Teachers' beliefs may be powerfully influenced (positively or negatively) by teachers' own experiences as learners (Holt Reynolds, 1992).

- Teachers' beliefs act as a **filter** through which teachers interpret new information and experience (Pajares, 1992).

- They interact bi-directionally with experience (i.e. beliefs influence practices and practices can also lead to changes in beliefs) (Richardson, 1996).

REVIEW OF LITERATURE (TEACHER BELIEF) (CONT.)

- Teachers' stated beliefs are <u>not</u> always a very reliable indication to reality (Pajares, 1992).

- Findings on the correspondence between the beliefs and practices are <u>contradictory</u> (Basturkmen, 2012).

- Research on the relationship between *beliefs* and *practices* can be characterized by three main positions;

$\implies$ **positive, weak, and no relationship**

REVIEW OF LITERATURE (TEACHER BELIEF) (CONT.)

Positive Relationship	Weak Relationship	No Relationship
Drive their *actions* and resistant to change (Borg, 2011)	Some *inconsistencies*, and a <u>tenuous</u> relationship (Basturkmen et al., 2004)	*Contextual factors* cause mismatches (Nishimuro & Borg, 2013)
Guide their *decision making* and what *learning opportunities* they provide for learners (Arnett & Turnbull, 2008; Borg & Al-Busaidi, 2012; Farrell & Lim, 2005)	*Experienced* teachers' mostly match, but sometime they *diverge* (Farrell & Bennis, 2013)	A <u>dilemma</u> of following beliefs or doing what can be done given the *practical constraints* (Junqueira & Payant, 2015)
Outweigh the effects of <u>teacher</u> <u>education</u> in influencing what teachers do in the classroom (Kagan, 1992; Richardson, 1996)	Evident to *some extent* in their classroom practices (Farrell & Ives, 2014)	"**teaching the test**" rather than "teaching the subject matter" (Melketo, 2012)

METHODOLOGY

• The study will adopt a <u>Phenomenological</u> Approach

What is Phenomenology?

Discovering and interpreting characteristics of a particular phenomenon as they truly are, or as they appear to the participants (Gall et al., 2007).

Gathers 'deep' information and perceptions through inductive, qualitative methods (interviews, discussions and participant observation), and represents it from the perspective of the research participants (Lester, 1999).

Why Phenomenology?

1. Examines the *nature* and *meaning* of teacher feedback as it is experienced by English language teachers.

2. Through phenomenology, teachers' *voices* on their beliefs about IF can be heard (Bogda & Biklen, 2007).

Investigating teachers' beliefs through phenomenology contributes to the field of teacher belief research by '*making the invisible visible*' (Laverty, 2003).

For teacher researchers, it provides opportunities to identify *tacit* teacher beliefs on various classroom practices (El-Okda, 2005).

The Qualitative Aspect

- Primarily a **Qualitative** Self Report Study

➤ Knowing how people interpret their experiences, how they construct their worlds, and what meaning they attribute to their experiences (Merriam, 2009).

➤ Given the interpretive nature of teacher belief research, it is strongly aligned with a **qualitative design**; it allows for in-depth and contextualized interpretation of teachers' beliefs and cognition (Borg, 2012).

A Quantitative Aspect

But for observing IF in practice, limited statistical analysis will also be used to count the *frequency* and *type* of IF.

PARTICIPANTS & CONTEXT

- **Participants:**

Five New Zealand English language teachers teaching ESL classes in New Zealand and **five** Iranian English language teachers instructing EFL classes in Iran (*upper intermediate* or *advanced level*)

- Pilot Study: **two** English language teachers

- Purposive Sampling

- **Context:**

New Zealand: Language schools

Iran: University of Isfahan Language Centre, Pooyesh Language School

RELATIONSHIP BETWEEN RQS AND METHODS

Research Questions	Main Data Collection Methods
RQ1. What **beliefs** do (a) Iranian EFL and (b) NZ ESL teachers hold about IF?	**First Interview (elicitation interview + cued response scenarios)**
RQ2. How do (a) Iranian EFL and (b) NZ ESL teachers **practice** IF?	**Classroom Observations + Field Notes**
RQ3. How do Iranian EFL & NZ ESL teachers **compare** with regard to IF beliefs and practices?	**Classroom Observations + First Interview + Second Interview**
RQ4,5. To what **extent** is there a match/mismatch between teachers' beliefs and classroom practices on IF? What **factors** could have contributed to any mismatch?	**Second Interview (stimulated recall) + Researcher's Interpretations**

INSTRUMENTS

1. Two Classroom Observations

2. First Interview (elicitation interview & cued response scenarios)

3. Second Interview (semi-structured interview & stimulated recalls)

INSTRUMENTS (CONT.)

1. Classroom Observations

- Using a coded observation schedule to note the *frequency* and *types* of feedback the teacher uses

- Field notes: provide information on the classroom events as they occur and the *context* in which IF occurs, and the researcher's thoughts and reflections on teachers' feedback types

- The researcher has a *non-participant* observation

- **Two** classroom observations for each teacher

INSTRUMENTS (CONT.)

2. First Interview *(elicitation interview & cued response scenarios)*

- **a)** Elicitation interview: Teachers will be asked closed and open ended questions related to effective teacher feedback, and in particular IF.

Examples

1. Tell me about a successful oral error correction you've recently done in your classroom?

2. Please complete these sentences in your own words:

During student's speaking, there are times when they make grammatical mistakes and I …..

INSTRUMENTS (CONT.)

b) <u>Cued Response Scenarios:</u> A number of typical classroom situations concerning IF will be provided to the teacher to comment on. The teacher will be asked to comment on what she would do had she been in that particular classroom situation.

Example

Please state what you think you should *do* in each of the following situations and *why*.

You have asked a student to look at a picture about food and quantities and describe what she sees.

The students says: There is <u>much</u> milk in the fridge.

INSTRUMENTS (CONT.)

3. Second Interview *(semi-structured interview & stimulated recalls)*

> <u>Stimulated recall:</u> The use of a stimulus (e.g. video or audio recordings) to help participants recall their thought processes at a particular time of a behaviour (Gass & Mackey, 2000).

> Teachers will be shown recordings of their classroom teaching and will be asked to *comment* on them with regards to their error correction frequency and techniques.

> Will be carried out within a *short time interval* from the classroom observation (up to 48 hours).

DATA COLLECTION PROCEDURE

Same Day → 1-2 days →

2 Classroom Observations	First Interview	Second Interview
Use of video recording & field notes	Use of semi-structured interview & cued response scenarios	Use of stimulated recall
(IF practices)	(IF beliefs)	(relationship between beliefs and practices)

DATA ANALYSIS

RQs	Data Analysis Methods
RQ1. What **beliefs** do (a) Iranian EFL and (b) NZ ESL teachers hold about IF?	Qualitative Analysis Methods (Organizing the data, reading the data and note taking, coding the data, identifying emerging themes, interpreting the data and visually representing the data (Creswell, 2013)).
RQ2. How do (a) Iranian EFL and (b) NZ ESL teachers **practice** IF?	*Pearson's Chi-square* analysis for frequency counts of the IF types Qualitative analysis of classroom transcriptions and field notes
RQ3. How do Iranian EFL & NZ ESL teachers **compare** with regard to IF beliefs and practices?	*Constant Comparative Method*; a method that allows for comparison of qualitative data.
RQ4,5. To what **extent** is there a match/mismatch between teachers' beliefs and classroom practices on IF? What **factors** could have contributed to any mismatch?	Researcher's interpretations of the second interview

TRIANGULATION

- Triangulation refers to the use of *multiple methods* or *data sources* in qualitative research to develop a comprehensive understanding of phenomena (Patton, 1999), and produce more **robust** data.

- **Data Triangulation:** Observational data + Self report data

beliefs
- elicitation interview
- cued response scenarios

practice
- observations
- field notes
- semi-structured interview
- stimulated recall

TRUSTWORTHINESS

- **Lincoln and Guba's (1985) Criteria for Trustworthiness:**

Established research methods
➢ Adopt well established research methods successfully used in previous similar studies (e.g. Basturkmen et al., 2004; Mackey et al., 2007; Mori, 2011; Nishimuro & Borg, 2013)
Inter-coder reliability (Mackey & Gass, 2005)   ➢ Will be looking at consistency in the coding of observational data
Triangulation
Members' check
Audit trail

ETHICAL CONSIDERATIONS

- This study will follow the regulations of **AUTEC**.

- The principles of <u>partnership</u>, <u>participation</u> and <u>protection</u> will be implemented throughout.

- Anonymizing the participants' names

- No judgements on teachers' practices

TIMETABLE FOR COMPLETION

Activities	Date
Complete first full draft of literature review	December 2015 – April 2016
PGR9 presentation	March 2016
Ethics application submitted	May 2016
Complete first full draft of methodology chapter	July 2016
Pilot study data collection and analysis	August – October 2016
Main study data collection and analysis	November 2016 – July 2017
Write results chapter	August – October 2017
Write discussion chapter	November – December 2017
Finalise write up: current literature update, introduction, conclusion, appendices	January – May 2018

KEY REFERENCES

Borg, S. (2003). Teacher cognition in language teaching: A review of research on what language teachers think, know, believe, and do. *Language Teaching, 36*(02), 81-109. doi:doi:10.1017/S0261444803001903

Borg, S. (2015). Researching language teacher education. *The Continuum companion to research methods in applied linguistics*.

Gass, S. M. (1997). *Input, Interaction, and the Second Language Learner*: Lawrence Erlbaum Associates.

Gass, S. M., & Mackey, A. (2000). *Stimulated recall methodology in second language research*: Routledge.

Mackey, A., Gass, S., & McDonough, K. (2000). How do learners perceive interactional feedback? *Studies in second language acquisition, 22*, 471-497.

Nassaji, H. (2015). *The Interactional Feedback Dimension in Instructed Second Language Learning: Linking Theory, Research, and Practice*: Bloomsbury Publishing.

Thank You

APPENDIX D

Typical Guidelines for the Submission of Manuscripts to Journals for Publication

1 All manuscripts should conform to the requirements of the Publication Manual of the American Psychological Association (always check the most recent edition). This can be accessed from the American Psychological Association.

2 Manuscripts should be written in a style that is accessible to a broad readership including those who may not be familiar with the subject matter.

3 This journal publishes manuscripts in seven categories: full length articles, forum, brief reports and summaries, teaching issues, research issues, research digest and book reviews. For the necessary submission items and other requirements, see the category below for the article you intend to submit. Authors are encouraged to read articles from the section to which they intend to submit to get an idea of the style and level of research required for publication.

4 This journal does not accept paper submissions. To submit a manuscript, please follow the online submission guidelines. First-time users will be asked to register. If a paper has more than one author, the person submitting the manuscript will have to identify the corresponding author and add the other authors using the "Add author' function. If you have questions about the submission process, please contact X.

5 This journal does not accept multiple simultaneous submissions from the same author because this practice monopolises reviewers' time. Multiple simultaneous submissions will be returned without review.

6 To facilitate the double-blind review process, please remove the author's name from the main text, the in-text citations, the reference list, and any running heads. Please replace the author's name with Author. If there are multiple authors, please use Author 1, Author 2, etc. Manuscripts submitted without author's name(s) removed will be returned without review for alteration and resubmission.

7 It is understood that submissions submitted to this journal have not been previously published and are not under consideration for publication elsewhere.
8 It is the author's responsibility to indicate to the editor the existence of any work already published (or under consideration for publication elsewhere) by the author(s) that is similar in content to the submitted manuscript.
9 It is also the author's responsibility to secure permission to reprint tables or figures that are used or adapted in the manuscript from another source. Written permission from the copyright holder is required before this journal can publish the material.
10 The editor of this journal reserves the right to make editorial changes in any manuscript accepted for publication to enhance clarity, concision, or style. The author will be consulted only if the editing has been substantial.
11 The editor's decisions are final.
12 The views expressed by contributors to this journal do not necessarily reflect those of the journal's editors or the editorial advisory board.
13 All authors of this journal receive a contributor's copy of the issue in which their work appears. In addition, the journal provides authors of full length articles a PDF copy of their article for their personal use.

[Given that there are seven submission categories, this Appendix D only refers to the information provided on the journal's website for the submission of full length articles.]

Full Length Articles

Full length articles typically present empirical research and analyse original data that the author has obtained using sound research methods. The journal publishes both quantitative and qualitative studies. Occasionally, this section features reflective articles (i.e. think pieces) that provide a comprehensive review of current knowledge in a specific area and present significant new directions for research.

Manuscripts should be no longer than 8,500 words including references, notes, tables and figures. Please indicate the number of words at the end of the article.

To submit a manuscript for a full length article, go to the online submission link. To facilitate the submission process, please have the following items at hand before you begin:

- Names and contact information for all authors
- Cover letter
- Abstract (300 words)
- Manuscript (8,500 words)
- Tables
- Figures
- Acknowledgements (if any)

If you have any questions about the submission process, please contact X.

APPENDIX E

Some of the Typical Reasons Journal Editors Reject Manuscripts before Seeking Reviews

1 The subject matter of the manuscript does not offer a novel and significant contribution to knowledge in the field.
2 There is an insufficiently compelling rationale for the research.
3 The literature review does not reveal the motivation for the research questions.
4 The subject matter is not a suitable fit for the readership of this journal.
5 The manuscript is more of an opinion piece than an empirical study.
6 A more persuasive case has to be built to justify the research questions and to bring out the contribution that the study can make to advance our knowledge of the field.
7 Key terms and constructs have not been adequately defined and this has led to claims that are not well supported.
8 The methodology of the study is under-reported so it is not possible to determine whether the findings as reported are valid and reliable.
9 The argument underpinning the study has not been clearly presented and has scarcely been referred to in the discussion of findings.
10 The manuscript would require substantial revision of form and content so because this exceeds the scope of the ordinary review process, we are unable to proceed with a consideration of this manuscript for publication.
11 There is a need to frame your research within the latest disciplinary conversations that will be familiar to readers of the target venue.
12 There are many language-related issues with the writing of this manuscript and these affect the clarity of meaning.
13 The methodology is very sketchy and each component needs to be clearly justified.
14 The findings do not align well with the framework and the research questions of the study.

Appendix E **157**

15 There is no discussion of the findings of the study reported in this manuscript and it is unclear how the claims and conclusions stated in the final section of the manuscript were informed by the findings of the study.

16 The subject matter of this manuscript would be of greater interest to local or regional readers than international readers.

17 There is a lack of alignment between the stated focus of the research in the introduction, the literature background focus, the wording of the research questions and the reported findings of the study.

18 It is unclear how all the collected data were analysed and which data were used to answer which research questions.

19 Readers need to be able to follow how the research was conducted at each stage of the process but there is insufficient descriptive detail to show exactly how the process unfolded.

20 The listing of different theoretical perspectives has not been used to discuss why the findings of your study arose as reported.

21 The data of this study seems to have come from a number of different sources but it is unclear (1) which data from which sources was drawn upon to answer some of the research questions and (2) how the data were triangulated as you say it was.

22 While the identification of a research gap may be a solid reason for a piece of research, you need to argue why it is an important gap for the field, that is, why it needs to be investigated and reported in the international literature.

23 Your manuscript has exceeded the word limit of 8,000 words for full length articles by 7,000 words.

24 Readers of this journal are certainly interested in pedagogical findings but they are equally interested in those that arise specifically from the reported findings of the research.

25 The data presented in this study are quite limited so this casts doubt over the strength of the claims you make in your discussion section. As a result, the conclusions you draw need in some cases to be hedged a lot more and in other cases revised because they simply over-state what the research has reported. This appears to be a pilot study and as such might be more suitable for publication in a more local journal.

26 The international readership of this journal is unlikely to be interested in reading about your context of study unless you can explain why context might be similar to other contexts. As it stands, this manuscript is not suitable for our international audience.

27 The findings of this study do advance our knowledge of one of the variables you investigated but overall the findings of the study make only a limited contribution as new knowledge to the field of second language writing.

28 It is unclear how you have operationalised language accuracy and language development in your study. This means it is not clear whether the data you have collected is valid for these two constructs and therefore whether the findings and the conclusions are valid.

REFERENCES

Allison, D., Cooley, L., Lewkowicz, J., & Nunan, D. (1998). Dissertation writing in action: The development of a dissertation writing support program for ESL graduate research students. *English for Specific Purposes,* 17, 199–217.

Andrews, R. (1995). *Teaching and learning argument.* London, NY: Cassell.

Auckland University of Technology. (2017). Code of practice for supervisors and student responsibilities. In *Auckland University of Technology Postgraduate handbook* (pp. 53–55 & pp. 56–57).

Basturkmen, H., & Bitchener, J. (2005). The text and beyond: Exploring the expectations of the academic community for the discussion of results section of Masters theses. *New Zealand Studies in Applied Linguistics,* 11, 1–20.

Basturkmen, H., East, M., & Bitchener, J. (2014). Supervisors' on-script feedback comments on drafts of dissertations: Socialising students into the Academic Discourse Community. *Teaching in Higher Education.* http://dx.doi/10.1080/13562517.2012.752728

Benesch, S. (2000). *Critical English for academic purposes: Theory, politics and practice.* Mahwah, NJ: Lawrence Erlbaum.

Bitchener, J. (2010). *Writing an Applied Linguistics thesis or dissertation: A guide to presenting empirical research.* Houndsmill, UK: Palgrave Macmillan.

Bitchener, J. (2012). A reflection on 'the language learning potential' of written CF. *Journal of Second Language Writing,* 21, 348–363.

Bitchener, J. (2015). *Feedback practices and motivations of AL thesis/dissertation supervisors in NZ, Australia, USA and UK: A self-report study.* A paper presented at Macquarie University, NSW, Australia on 15 September, 2015, as part of the Linguistics Research Seminars.

Bitchener, J. (2016). The content feedback practices of Applied Linguistics supervisors in New Zealand and Australian universities. *ARAL,* 39, 105–121.

Bitchener, J., & Basturkmen, H. (2006). Perceptions of the difficulties of postgraduate L2 thesis students writing the discussion section. *Journal of English for Academic Purposes,* 5, 4–18.

References **159**

Bitchener, J., & Ferris, D. (2012). *Written corrective feedback in second language acquisition and writing*. New York: Routledge.

Bitchener, J., & Storch, N. (2016). *Written corrective feedback for L2 development*. Bristol: Multilingual Matters.

Bitchener, J., Basturkmen, H., & East, M. (2010). The focus of supervisor feedback to thesis/dissertation students. *International Journal of English Studies*, 11, 79–97.

Cadman, K. (1997). Thesis writing for international students: A question of identity. *English for Specific Purposes*, 16, 3–14.

Casanave, C., & Hubbard, P. (1992). The writing assignments and writing problems of doctoral students: Faculty perceptions, pedagogical issues, and needed research. *English for Specific Purposes*, 11, 33–49.

Casanave, C., & Li, X. (Eds). (2008). *Learning the literacy practices of graduate school: Insiders' reflections on academic enculturation*. Ann Arbor, MI: The University of Michigan Press.

Cooley, L., & Lewkowicz, J. (1995). The writing needs of graduate students at the University of Hong Kong: A project report. *Hong Kong Papers in Linguistics and Language Teaching*, 18, 121–123.

Cooley, L., & Lewkowicz, J. (1997). Developing awareness of the rhetorical and linguistic conventions of writing a thesis in English: Addressing the needs of ESL/EFL postgraduate students. In A. Duszak (Ed.), *Culture and styles of academic discourse* (pp. 113–140). Berlin: Mouton de Gruyter.

Cooley, L., & Lewkowicz, J. (2003). *Dissertation writing in practice: Turning ideas into text*. Hong Kong: Hong Kong University Press.

Cresswell, J. (2009). *Research design: Qualitative, quantitative and mixed methods approaches*. London: Sage.

Dong, Y. (1998). Non-native graduate students' thesis/dissertation writing in science: Self reports by students and their advisors from two US institutions. *English for Specific Purposes*, 17, 369–390.

Dornyei, Z. (2007). *Research methods in Applied Linguistics: Quantitative, qualitative and mixed methodologies*. Oxford, UK: Oxford University Press.

East, M., Bitchener, J., & Basturkmen, H. (2012). What constitutes effective feedback on postgraduate students' writing? The students' perspective. *Journal of University Teaching and learning Practice*, 9(2), 1–16. Article 7. http://ro.uow.edu.au/jutlp/vol9/iss2/7

Finch, G. (2000). *Linguistic terms and concepts*. London: Macmillan.

Frost, A. (1999). Supervision of NESB postgraduate students in science-based disciplines. In Y. Ryan & O. Zuber-Skerritt (Eds), *Supervising postgraduates from non-English speaking backgrounds* (pp. 101–109). Birmingham, UK: Open University Press.

Hyland, K. (2000). *Disciplinary discourses: Social interactions in academic writing*. London: Longman.

Hyland, K. (2007). *Genre and second language writing*. Ann Arbor: University of Michigan Press.

Hyland, K. (2009). *Academic discourse*. London: Continuum.

Hyland, K., & Tse, P. (2004). Metadiscourse in academic writing: A reappraisal. *Applied Linguistics*, 25, 156–177.

James, K. (1984). The writing of theses by speakers of English as a foreign language: A case study. In R. Williams, J. Swales, & J. Kirkman (Eds), *Common ground: Shared interests in ESP and communication studies, ELT documents 117* (pp. 99–113). Oxford: Pergamon Press.

160 References

Jenkins, S., Jordan, M., & Weiland, P. (1993). The role of writing in graduate engineering education: A survey of faculty beliefs and practices. *English for Specific Purposes*, 12, 51–67.

Kumar, V., & Stracke, E. (2007). An analysis of written feedback on a PhD thesis. *Teaching in Higher Education*, 12, 461–470.

Mackey, A., & Gass, S. (2005). *Second language research: Methodology and design*. London: Lawrence Erlbaum Associates.

Mitchell, R., Myles, R., & Marsden, E. (1998). *Second language learning theories*. London: Routledge.

O'Connell, F., & Jin, L. (2001). *A structural model of literature review: An analysis of Chinese postgraduate students' writing*. Paper presented at BALEAP Conference, Sheffield Hallam University, Sheffield, UK.

Ortega, L. (2009). *Understanding second language acquisition*. London: Hodder Education.

Paltridge, B., & Starfield, S. (2007). *Thesis and dissertation writing in a second language: A handbook for supervisors*. New York: Routledge.

Sofoulis, Z. (1997). *What scholar would endorse me? Transference, counter-transference and postgraduate pedagogy*. Paper presented at 3 October 1997 to the School of Education, the University of Auckland: Unpublished.

Toulmin, S., Reike, R., & Janik, A. (1984). *An introduction to reasoning*. New York: Macmillan.

INDEX

Note: *italic* page numbers indicate tables.

abstracts: argument creation 79–80; argument creation feedback 88; conference presentations *see* conference abstracts; content feedback 72–3; content selection 50–1; discourse move options 51, *51*, 79–80, 88; purposes/functions 50

advance organisers 90–1

alignment of questions and data sources 64–5

American Association for Applied Linguistics (AAAL), guidelines for conference abstracts 101–3

American Psychological Association (APA), conventions 68

Andrews, R. 75

APA conventions 68

argument, use of term 75

argument creation 43; abstract 79–80; abstract feedback 88; argument structures 75–80; conclusion chapter 79; conclusion chapter feedback 87–8; discussion of results 78–9; discussion of results chapter feedback 85–7; introduction chapter 76–7; introduction chapter feedback 80–2; literature review 76; literature review feedback 82–3; methodology chapter 77–8; methodology chapter feedback 83–4; overview 74;

post-writing feedback 80–8; pre-writing advice 74–80; results chapter 78; results chapter feedback 85; understanding 'argument' 75

argument overview 21–3; chapter argument vs. textbook content 74–5; as chapter writing strategy 52

argument structure, table of contents 19–21

argument structures 75–80

Basturkmen, H. 26, 121, 125–6, 126–8

Bitchener, J. 2, 38, 121, 122–4, 125–6, 126–8

book: aims 3; overview 1

book title recommendations, provisional enrolment 8

boxes: abstract purposes/functions 50; advance organisers 91; alignment of questions and data sources 64–5; argument overview 22–3; book title recommendations 9; clause structures 98; conclusion chapter purposes/ functions 49; conference abstracts 101–2; descriptive detail 63; discourse move options for conference abstracts 103; discussion of results purposes/ functions 48; focus of literature review feedback 34; initial research questions feedback 31; introduction

162 Index

chapter purposes/functions 39; journal
acceptance criteria 112–13; key
elements of confirmation proposal
28–9; key information on literature 18;
key stages in doctoral journey 12–13;
literature review purposes/functions
41–2; literature review sub-move
options 44; meaning connections/gaps
96–7; methodology chapter purposes/
functions 45; methodology/design 24;
methodology feedback 34;
mind-mapping 18–19; oral presentation
of proposal 28–9; paragraph coherence
94–5; philosophical approach statement
61–2; PowerPoint slides 20; PowerPoint
slides feedback 35–6; PowerPoint
slides for conference presentation 107;
profile of doctoral graduate 10–11;
rationale and significance feedback 35;
rationale and significance statement
24, 25–8; results chapter purposes/
functions 46; section conclusion 92, 93;
section headings 90; sentence length
99, 100; stages in drafting journal
article manuscript 110; sub-section
organisation 91; successful conference
abstract 104; summary of findings 70;
supervisor-student agreement 11–12;
table of contents 20; table presentation
and commentary 67; topic sentences
92–3; use of discourse markers/
connectors 95–6; verb tenses 98;
word choice 97

Casanave, C. 119–20
chapter content feedback: abstract
72–3; alignment of questions and data
sources 64–5; amount of literature
59; conclusion chapter 69–72;
content balance 56; content selection
58–9; context of research problem 56;
contribution to the field 72; critical
engagement 59–60; data analysis 65;
descriptive detail 62–3; discussion of
results 68–9; discussion points 68; final
remarks 72; findings chapter 65–8;
formatting 68; hierarchical ordering of
findings 66; introduction chapter 54–8;
justification of method 63; limitations
of study 71; linking to wider literature
68–9; literature review 58–60; location
of explanation and discussion 65–6;
making claims and drawing conclusions
71; means of investigation 57;

methodology areas not covered 60–2;
methodology chapter 60–5; nature
and scope of research problem 55; oral
feedback 69; organisation of findings
66; originality and significance 57;
overview 54; personal voice 57–8;
practice applications 71; rationale and
significance components 55–6; research
recommendations 71; summary of
findings 69–70; tables and figures 66–7
chapter content selection: abstract 50–1;
conclusion chapter 49–50; discussion
of results 47–9; introduction chapter
39–41; literature review 41–4;
methodology chapter 45–6; overview
37–8; results chapter 46–7; role of
genre knowledge 38
chapter writing strategies: argument
overview 52; chapter deconstruction
51–3; iterations 53; table of contents 52
clause structures 98–9
code of practice 130–3
coherence: macro level 90–2; meaning
connections/gaps 96–7; overview
89–90; paragraphs 93; section
conclusion 92; within sections 92–3;
within sentences 97–100; sub-section
organisation 91; syntax 97–8; use of
discourse markers/connectors 95–6;
vocabulary 97–8
cohort/pot luck meetings 4; chapter
deconstruction 52; oral presentation of
proposal 28–9
conclusion chapter: argument creation
79; argument creation feedback
87–8; chapter content feedback
69–72; chapter content selection
49–50; contribution to the field 72,
87; discourse move options 50, 50, 79;
findings chapter 72; limitations of study
71, 88; making claims and drawing
conclusions 71; practice applications
71; purposes/functions 49; research
recommendations 71; summary of
findings 69–70, 87
conference abstracts: AAAL guidelines
101–3; deconstruction 104; discourse
move options 103; vs. dissertation/
article abstracts 103–4; successful
example 104–5; writing process 101–5
conference presentations 101–8; abstract
writing *see* conference abstracts; mock
presentation 108; PowerPoint slides
105–8; presentation for publication 108

Index   **163**

confirmation proposal *see* research
     proposal advice
connectors, use of 95–6
constructs, defining 40
content balance, introduction chapter 56
content selection, literature review
     58–9, 83
context of research problem 56
contribution to the field: chapter content
     feedback 72; conclusion chapter
     feedback 87
Cooley, L. 119–20
creation of argument 43
critical engagement 59–60
critical evaluation, feedback 83

data analysis: chapter content feedback 65;
     presentation 77
deconstruction: literature review 43; of
     model chapters 51–2
defining terms and constructs, argument
     creation feedback 80–1
dependency, levels of 2
descriptive detail 62–3
dictionaries 89
discourse markers, use of 95–6
discourse move options 38; abstract 51,
     51, 79–80, 88; conclusion chapter
     50, *50*, 79; conference abstracts 103;
     discussion of results 48–9, *48*, 78–9,
     85–7; introduction chapter 40–1, *41*,
     76–7; literature review 42–4, *42*, 76;
     methodology chapter 45–6, *46*, 77–8;
     results chapter *47*, 78
discussion chapter *see* discussion of results
discussion of results: argument creation
     78–9; argument creation feedback
     85–7; chapter content feedback
     68–9; chapter content selection
     47–9; discourse move options 48–9, *48*,
     78–9, 86; discussion in wider context
     86–7; discussion points 68; extent
     of discussion 86; linking to wider
     literature 68–9; location of 65–6; oral
     feedback 69; purposes/functions 47–8
discussion points 68
dissertation overview, introduction
     chapter feedback 82
doctoral graduates: key stages in doctoral
     journey 12–13; profile of 10–11
Dong, Y. 120

East, M. 121, 125–6, 126–8
explanation of findings, location of 65–6

feasibility 32–3
figures, chapter content feedback 66–7
final remarks, chapter content feedback 72
Finch, G. 89
findings chapter *see* results chapter
formatting, findings chapter 68

Gass, S. 22
genre, defining 38
genre knowledge, role of 38
global study 122–4

headings 90
hierarchical ordering of findings 66
Hubbard, P. 119–20
Hyland, K. 72, 121
hypothesis drafting 30–1

initial action plan: argument overview
     21–3; key elements of proposal 16;
     literature mind-map 17–19; literature
     record 17, *18*; literature review for
     proposal 16–17; methodology/
     design 23–4; PowerPoint slides 28–9;
     proposal questionnaire 15–16; rationale
     and significance components 24–8;
     research proposal advice 15–29; table of
     contents 19–21
institutional support, for students and
     supervisors 3
introduction chapter: argument creation
     76–7; argument creation feedback
     80–2; chapter content feedback
     54–8; chapter content selection
     39–41; content balance 56; context of
     research problem 56; defining terms
     and constructs 80–1; discourse move
     options 40–1, *41*, 76–7; dissertation
     overview 82; literature detail 81; means
     of investigation 57; nature and scope of
     research problem 55; niche occupation
     82; originality and significance 57;
     personal voice 57–8; rationale and
     significance components 55–6, 81–2;
     writing process 54–5
iterations: as chapter writing strategy 53;
     of chapters 7

James, K. 120
Janik, A. 75
journal articles: acceptance criteria
     112–13; areas of weakness 113–18;
     conclusion weaknesses 118; discussion
     weaknesses 117; focus of article 109;

164 Index

introduction weaknesses 113–14; journal responses 111; journal selection 109; key stages 109–12; literature review weaknesses 114–15; methodology weaknesses 115–16; overview 108; proofreading 112; publication 112; rejections 156–7; results/findings weaknesses 116–17; review and revision 110; revision and resubmission 111; stages in drafting 109–10; submission 110–11; submission guidelines 154–5
justification of method 63, 77, 84

key stages in doctoral journey 12–13
knowledge critique 43
knowledge territory 43

learning support services 3
level of detail, methodology chapter 45–6
Lewkowicz, J. 119–20
limitations of study: argument creation feedback 88; chapter content feedback 71
literature, critical assessment 40–1
literature mind-map 17–19, 76
literature record *18*
literature review: amount of literature 59; argument creation 76; argument creation feedback 82–3; chapter content selection 41–4; content selection 58–9, 83; critical engagement 59–60; critical evaluation 83; deconstruction 43; discourse move options 42–4, *42*, 76; iterations 7; purposes/functions 41–2; writing process 58
location of explanation and discussion 65–6

Manchester University study 120
meaning connections/gaps, coherence 96–7
means of investigation 57
meetings: cohort/pot luck 4; group discussions 79; oral presentation of proposal 28–9
meta-text 22, 78, 79
meta-textual information 47
methodology chapter: alignment of questions and data sources 64–5; areas not covered 60–2; argument creation 77–8; argument creation feedback 83–4; chapter content feedback 60–5;

chapter content selection 45–6; data analysis 65; descriptive detail 62–3; discourse move options 45–6, *46*, 77–8; justification of method 63, 84; philosophical approach statement 61–2; procedural gaps 84; purposes/functions 45; writing process 60
methodology/design, research proposal advice 23–4
mind-mapping, literature 17–19, 76
mock presentations 108

nature and scope of research problem, chapter content feedback 55
New Zealand feedback study 125–6
niche, establishment and occupation 40–1, 42, 82

oral feedback 69
oral presentation of proposal 28–9, 35–6
organisation of findings 66
original contribution 39
originality 33; chapter content feedback 57
other texts: overview 101; *see also* conference presentations; journal articles

paragraphs, coherence 93–7
parameters, identification and justification 39
passive voice 22
personal voice 57–8
philosophical approach statement 61–2, 77
philosophical discussion, methodology chapter 45
post-writing feedback: argument creation 80–8; defining 5–6; focus of 6–7; overview 3, 30; pre-enrolment feedback 30; sources of 6; timing of 6–7; *see also* provisional enrolment
pot-luck meetings 4
PowerPoint slides: conference presentations 105–8; mock presentation 108; oral presentation of proposal 28–9; research proposal feedback 35–6; sample presentation 134–53; table of contents 20–1
practice applications, chapter content feedback 71
pre-confirmation advice: argument overview 21–3; key elements of proposal 16; key stages in doctoral

journey 12–13; literature mind-map 17–19; literature record 17, *18*; literature review for proposal 16–17; methodology/design 23–4; oral presentation of proposal 28–9; profile of doctoral graduate 10–11; proposal questionnaire 15–16; rationale and significance components 24–8; research proposal advice 15–29; supervisor-student agreement 11–12; table of contents 19–21; timing of stages 13–14; understanding of post-graduate study 10

pre-writing advice: argument creation 74–80; defining 4; nature of 5; overview 3; sources of 4; timing of 5; *see also* provisional enrolment

procedural gaps, methodology chapter 84

profile of doctoral graduate 10–11

proposal questionnaire 15–16

provisional enrolment: advice before enrolment 8–9; argument overview 21–3; book title recommendations 8; key elements of proposal 16; key stages in doctoral journey 12–13; literature mind-map 17–19; literature record 17, *18*; literature review for proposal 16–17; methodology/design 23–4; oral presentation of proposal 28–9; overview 8; post-writing feedback 30–6; pre-confirmation advice 10–29; profile of doctoral graduate 10–11; proposal questionnaire 15–16; rationale and significance components 24–8; research proposal advice 9, 15–29; supervisor-student agreement 11–12; table of contents 19–21; timing of stages 13–14; understanding of post-graduate study 10

published research: argument construction feedback 121; content organisation 120–1; global study 122–4; linguistic accuracy feedback 122; nature and focus of feedback 121–2; New Zealand feedback study 125–6; overview 119; purposes/functions of feedback 121; student perspective 126–8; subject knowledge feedback 121; summary 129; supervisor perceptions of student difficulties 119–20

purposes/functions: abstract 50; conclusion chapter 49; of feedback 121; introduction chapter 39–40; literature review 41–2; methodology chapter 45; results chapter 46

rationale and significance components: chapter content feedback 55–6; introduction chapter feedback 81–2; research proposal advice 24–8

record keeping, literature record 17, *18*

Reike, R. 75

replication 46, 77

reported difficulties, supervisors and students 1–2

research problem: context of 56; nature and scope 55

research proposal advice: argument overview 21–3; initial action plan 15–29; initial proposal feedback 30–3; key elements of proposal 16; literature record 17, *18*; literature review for proposal 16–17; methodology/design component 23–4; oral presentation 28–9; proposal questionnaire 15–16; provisional enrolment 9, 15–29; rationale and significance components 24–8; research and writing strategies 16; table of contents 19–21

research proposal feedback: accuracy and completeness 32; confirmation proposal 33–6; feasibility 32–3; importance of area of focus 32; initial proposal 30–3; literature review 33–4; methodology section 34; originality 33; PowerPoint slides 35–6; proposal focus 30–1; rationale and significance components 35

research recommendations, feedback 71

research territory 40

results chapter: argument creation 78; argument creation feedback 85; chapter content feedback 65–8; chapter content selection 46–7; discourse move options 47, 78; explanation vs. discussion 85; formatting 68; hierarchical ordering 66; level of explanation 85; location of explanation and discussion 65–6; organisation of findings 66; purposes/functions 46; tables and figures 66–7

role of genre knowledge 38

section conclusion 92, 93

sections, coherence within 92–3

sentences: coherence 97–100; length 99–100

significance, chapter content feedback 57

significance and rational components, research proposal advice 24–8

166 Index

Sofoulis, Z. 121
stages of doctoral study, timing of 13–14
Stanford University study 119
student perspective 126–8
students: institutional support 3; reported
difficulties 2; *see also* code of practice
sub-section organisation 91
supervisor-student agreement 11–12
supervisors: institutional support 3;
reported difficulties 1–2; subject
knowledge 59; *see also* code of
practice
syntax, and coherence 97–100

table of contents: argument overview 75;
chapter writing strategies 52; initial
creation 19–21; PowerPoint slides 20–1
tables, chapter content feedback 66–7
terms, defining 40

timing: of post-writing feedback 6–7; of
pre-writing advice 5; of stages 13–14
topic sentences 92–3
Toulmin, S. 75

units of content 38
University of Hong Kong study 119
USA universities study 120

verbs: choice of 97; tenses 98
vocabulary, and coherence 97–8
voices, active/passive 22

word choice 97
writer's voice 57–8
writing challenges 1–3
writing process: introduction chapter 54–5;
literature review 58; methodology
chapter 60; strategies 51–3